Jump Start Adobe XD

by Daniel Schwarz

Product Manager: Simon Mackie

English Editor: Katie Monk

Technical Editor: Darin Dimitrov

Cover Designer: Alex Walker

Published by SitePoint Pty. Ltd.

48 Cambridge Street Collingwood
VIC Australia 3066
Web: www.sitepoint.com
Email: books@sitepoint.com

I978-0-9953826-1-9 (print)

ISBN 978-0-9953827-3-2 (ebook)
Printed and bound in the United States of America

About Daniel Schwarz

Daniel Schwarz is the founder of Airwalk Studios and co-editor of the Design & UX channel at SitePoint. When he's not cooking, travelling the world or experiencing new cultures, he's working remotely as a designer, coder, writer, author, and digital nomad.

About SitePoint

SitePoint specializes in publishing fun, practical, and easy-to-understand content for web professionals. Visit http://www.sitepoint.com/ to access our blogs, books, newsletters, articles, and community forums. You'll find a stack of information on JavaScript, PHP, Ruby, mobile development, design, and more.

To my wife, for putting up with all of my late nights.

Table of Contents

Chapter 2   Learning the Basics with Low-Fidelity Prototyping

Chapter 3   Prototyping User Flows and

Receiving Feedback..38

Chapter 4 Getting Visual with the Property Inspector...66

Chapter 5   Hi-Fi Prototyping With Symbols

and Repeat Grids...100

Appendix A   Accelerating Workflows with

Keyboard Shortcuts..145

Preface

Adobe Experience Design CC (otherwise known as Adobe XD[1], for short) is a minimalist desktop app for designers that need to:

1. Design user interfaces
2. Prototype user flows and interactions
3. Export image assets for the development of apps and websites

While you can accomplish all three of these things (in one way or another) using the two biggest design apps on the market today – Photoshop[2] and Sketch[3] – Adobe XD is the only tool to offer design and prototyping functionality *natively*, and that's why it's quickly becoming a top contender in the design space.

Adobe XD is everything a designer needs, right out of the box.

Why Adobe XD Exists

Bohemian Coding built Sketch because user-interface designers needed a design application that was focused on the needs of user-interface designers. Since Adobe Photoshop is a multi-disciplinary design tool (it was originally aimed at photographers), the app had an abundance of features that weren't relevant to user-interface designers. However, while Sketch simplified the designing experience, its makers neglected to create a Windows version of the app, nor include any prototyping tools (Sketch requires third-party *plugins* for this).

Adobe built Adobe XD to re-enter the competition – by offering the same minimalist experience as Sketch, but with added tools that Sketch is yet to introduce (ie, prototyping tools), *and* by releasing a Windows version (which Bohemian Coding said it would never do). It's assumed that even Adobe recommends that user-interface designers should switch from Adobe Photoshop to Adobe XD – but what about Sketch users? Let's take a quick look.

---

[1] http://www.adobe.com/products/experience-design.html
[2] http://www.photoshop.com/
[3] https://sketchapp.com/

Photoshop vs. Sketch vs. Adobe XD

Choosing an app isn't about which one is *best*. It comes down to your individual needs, and what you're already familiar with.

Photoshop, for example, is very multi-disciplinary, and many of the tools are aimed at photography experts and those who need to manipulate bitmap images. UI designers simply don't need most of the features that Photoshop offers, which is why Adobe sought to create a desktop app dedicated to crafting user interfaces.

Sketch, on the other hand, is specifically aimed at UI designers, but isn't available for Windows, nor does it offer prototyping tools natively, both of which Adobe XD does. Sketch users must download *plugins* to extend their workflow. So if you're already a happy user of InVision, Marvel, or some other kind of prototyping tool that integrates with Sketch, *and* you're a macOS user, then you might be better suited to Sketch.

If you're a macOS user and you think Sketch could also be a contender for your design workflow, then check out my book *Jump Start Sketch*.[4]

Figma[5] is another tool that's been gaining some traction lately. It's a user-interface design tool for both Windows and macOS, but again, without prototyping tools. Now we know more about these design tools, I think we should summarise them:

	Platform	Focus on UI	Prototyping tools
Photoshop	Windows/macOS	No	Plugin only
Sketch	macOS	Yes	Plugin only
Figma	Windows/macOS	Yes	No
Adobe XD	Windows/macOS	Yes	Yes

So Who Should Read Jump Start Adobe XD?

Jump Start Adobe XD is for:

---

[4] https://www.sitepoint.com/premium/books/jump-start-sketch

[5] https://www.figma.com/

- Designers with an Adobe CC subscription who want to switch from Photoshop to a tool more focused on user-interface design
- Designers who want to combine design and prototyping tools into a single app to improve their workflow and productivity
- Curious designers who want to see if Adobe XD can replace their current design tool without taking up too much time
- Beginner-level designers keen to kickstart their learning

Conventions Used

You'll notice that we've used certain typographic and layout styles throughout this book to signify different types of information. Look out for the following items.

Tips, Notes, and Warnings

Hey, You!

Tips provide helpful little pointers.

Ahem, Excuse Me ...

Notes are useful asides that are related—but not critical—to the topic at hand. Think of them as extra tidbits of information.

Make Sure You Always ...

... pay attention to these important points.

Watch Out!

Warnings highlight any gotchas that are likely to trip you up along the way.

Supplementary Materials

- https://www.sitepoint.com/community/ are SitePoint's forums, for help on any tricky web problems.
- **books@sitepoint.com** is our email address, should you need to contact us to report a problem, or for any other reason.
- The book's file archive[6], which contains support files that will be used in the book.

[6.] https://github.com/spbooks/jsadobexd1

Chapter **1**

Getting Familiar with the UI

In the first chapter of this book we'll familiarise ourselves with the XD interface before taking a very hands-on approach to low-fidelity prototyping. All of the screenshots in this book are taken from the macOS version of Adobe XD. However, the walkthroughs (and shortcuts) are applicable to Windows, too.

If you're switching from Sketch, you'll notice many similarities in Adobe XD (both visually and in terms of features). Although if you're switching from Photoshop, Adobe XD will still *feel* like an Adobe app in some ways, even if it doesn't look like it, or some of the features seem a little unfamiliar to you.

Here's a swift comparison of XD (above) and Sketch (below).

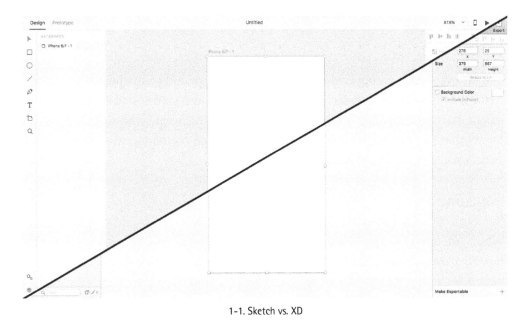

1-1. Sketch vs. XD

Before We Begin

You can download Adobe XD via Creative Cloud like any other Adobe app. So if you already have a Creative Cloud subscription, you're all set. If not, you can start your Creative Cloud trial on the Adobe website[7].

Let's dive in.

 ### Adobe XD Is Still Under Active Development

It's worth noting that Adobe are actively developing XD. It is already a very versatile and powerful tool, but new features are continually being added in monthly updates. It is also important to note that, as of this writing, the Windows version of the app hasn't yet got all the features of the macOS version, but the Adobe team are working hard to get both versions on par. The best place to stay up-to-date with the latest XD developments is the official Adobe blog[8].

[7.] http://www.adobe.com/creativecloud.html

[8.] https://blogs.adobe.com/creativecloud/category/xd/

Workspace

Your workspace is comprised of an unlimited canvas and the artboards inside it. **Artboards** typically represent one webpage or one app screen in your design, where their size depends on the dimensions of the browser window or device screen that you're designing for. Your workspace can contain as many artboards as necessary, even if they're all different sizes.

Welcome Screen

When you open the app you'll see a welcome screen that asks you to specify what type of artboard you'd like to start with. It's commonplace to demonstrate what your design would look like on different desktop and device screens, effectively creating an adaptive design (that is, a design that adapts to the device/screen it's been viewed on). It's also widely accepted that you should start with the smallest-sized screen first (if you're designing for the web, this is known as a mobile-first approach to design).

Why Mobile-First

Why? Because designing on smaller screens forces you to design with simplicity in mind. It's much harder to scale down a design for smaller screens than it is to scale up a design for larger screens. If you were creating a responsive web design you would start with a mobile artboard and work up to tablets and then desktop screens. If you were designing an iOS app, you'd start with the smallest iPhone and work up to iPad, then iPad Pro.

Over the course of this book we'll be designing and prototyping an iOS app, so choose *iPhone 6/7* to start off.

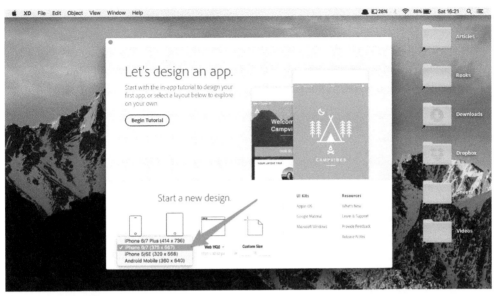

1-2. Welcome screen

Here's our very first artboard!

1-3. First artboard

Ready-Made UI Kits

Like Sketch, Adobe XD has three pre-made UI kits – Apple iOS, Google Material and Microsoft Windows. You can extract native OS design elements from these to use in your mockups, although we'll be focusing on designing a custom UI.

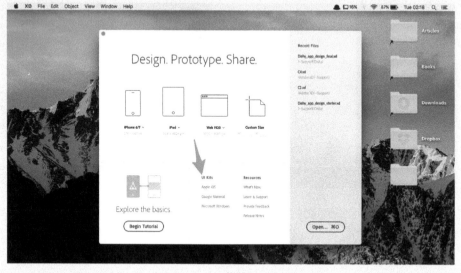

1-4. UI kits

Canvas

As I mentioned, the canvas is unlimited. All artboards will be visible on the canvas at once, making it easy to flip back-and-forth between the different screens. Any objects that aren't inside an artboard are automatically inserted into what's called the **pasteboard** – a separate artboard for scattered objects.

Artboards

When you need to create new artboards, tap **A** and select a device from the inspector on the right-hand side. If you need a custom-size artboard (maybe you'd like to have your app icons in the same document), tap **A** and draw out the artboard using the mouse, rather than select one from the inspector.

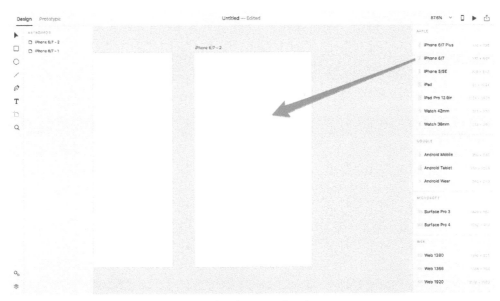

1-5. Creating new artboards

In some cases, your content will exceed the dimensions of the screen. If you select the artboard and drag the handles you'll be able to resize it, but you'll also notice a dashed, blue line, which indicates the boundaries of the viewport (the above-the-fold content). Anything below the fold is accessed by scrolling, which you can do when testing prototypes in real devices. We'll definitely explore that later in the book!

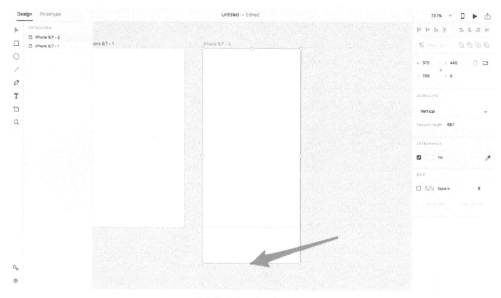

1-6. Resizing the viewport

You can change the viewport height at any time using the inspector, and you can also turn the viewport off completely if you don't want the screen to be scrollable in live preview mode.

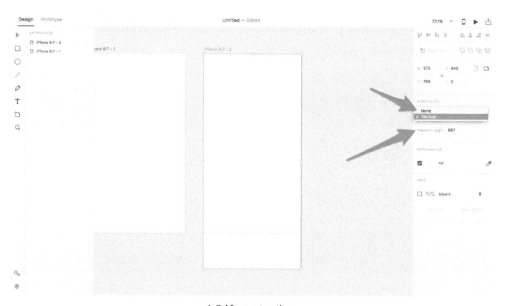

1-7. Viewport options

Over the course of the book we'll create many artboards, eventually wrapping up with the following end result:

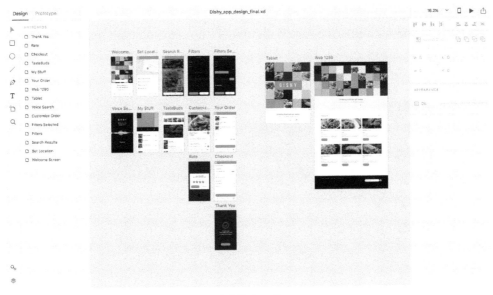

1-8. End result

Prototype Workspace

Adobe XD has an equally important secondary workspace called the *Prototype* workspace, and this is where we:

1. Link screens together with transitions
2. Create video demonstrations of our design
3. Prototype (test) the design in a browser or device
4. Share the prototype with teammates to request feedback

Prototyping is where Adobe XD outshines Photoshop and Sketch, and we'll be using this workspace almost as often as the *Design* workspace.

Prototyping isn't about throwing together a few fancy transitions to impress our clients and teammates; creating prototypes and testing them in real devices is integral to crafting exceptional UX. It helps us identify flaws that we wouldn't ordinarily discover by simply looking at the design.

Toolbar

As in Photoshop, the toolbar appears on the left-hand side, so let's run through the tools, along with their keyboard shortcuts (the same on both macOS and Windows):

- Move (**M**)
- Rectangle (**T**)
- Ellipse (**E**)
- Line (**L**)
- Pen (**P**)
- Text (**T**)
- Artboard (**A**)
- Zoom-In (**Z**)

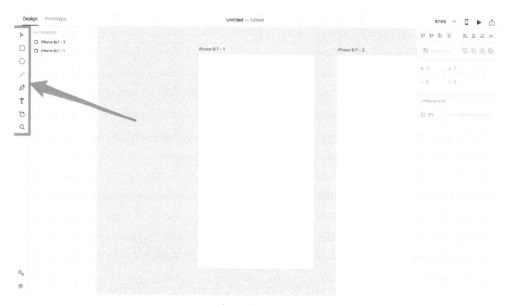

1-9. Accessing the toolbar

 Use the Shortcuts

I find that the zoom-in and zoom-out keyboard shortcuts are easier than using the zoom tool or the application toolbar, which are **Cmd +** and **Cmd -** on macOS and **Ctrl +** and **Ctrl -** on Windows.

Layer List

In Adobe XD, the layer list appears on the left-hand side when you use the keyboard shortcut **Cmd + Y (Ctrl + Y** in Windows), or when you click the layer list icon in the very bottom-left corner of the app window. Photoshop, by default, always displayed the layer list on the *right*-hand side, but Adobe took a little inspiration from Sketch on this one.

Layers are the smallest of components that make up your design. Layers can be shape layers, text layers, bitmap layers, etc.

1-10. Opening the layer list

It's here that you'll see a hierarchical tree of your artboards, groups and layers. But what makes this interface so special, compared with other design apps, is that the layer list only displays the contents of the currently selected artboard, which reduces distraction. You only see what you need to see.

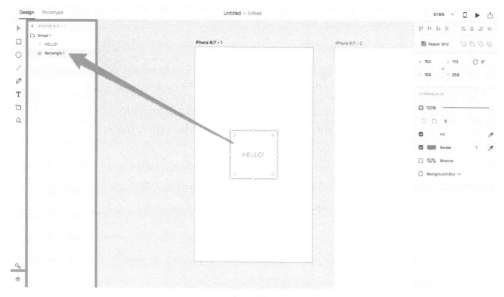

1-11. Layer hierarchy

Property Inspector

When you need to style layers, the inspector is your friend. It's here that you define your backgrounds, fills, borders, border radii, shadows, widths, heights, rotation degrees, and so on. You can also activate Repeat Grids from here, as well as specify alignments and boolean operations. As you may have seen earlier, there are settings unique to artboards and so only appear when an artboard is selected (and the same for text).

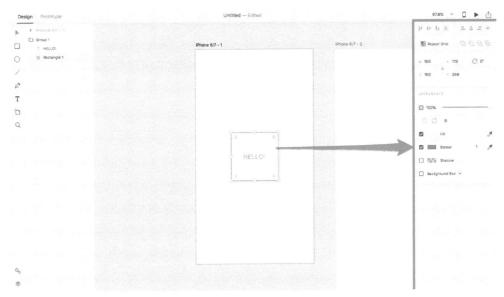

1-12. Accessing the inspector

Don't worry, we'll learn how to use all of these features in the following chapter.

Application Toolbar

Aside from the zoom dropdown, this toolbar mostly deals with prototyping tools. Here you can switch between the Design and Prototype workspaces, connect to a mobile device (for testing user flows and interactions), preview prototypes in Adobe XD itself, or share prototypes to receive feedback and comments.

In the six chapters to come, we're going to learn all about prototyping with Adobe XD, while designing a sample app. But if you're not into hands-on learning, you can still follow us on the journey using the screenshots in this book. It's **totally** up to you!

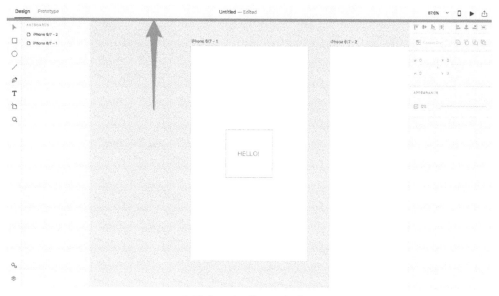

1-13. Accessing the app toolbar

Next: Learning the Basics with Low-Fidelity Prototyping

In the next chapter we'll dive straight into low-fidelity prototyping. Now that we're familiar with the UI of Adobe XD, we'll be learning how to use the basic design tools while digitally mocking up the rough idea for our app.

As mentioned earlier, the end result will contain various screens that will make up our finished app design. This app design will be based on Adobe XD's official iOS app, Dishy[9] — a location-based food-ordering app.

See you there!

---

9. https://helpx.adobe.com/experience-design/how-to/ux-tips-tricks.html

Chapter

2

Learning the Basics with Low-Fidelity Prototyping

In Chapter 1 we took a tour of Adobe XD, and even looked into the keyboard shortcuts of the most common tools. This should give us a good foundation to work with as we explore more of Adobe XD, then go on to design a low-fidelity mockup of an app.

Welcome Screen

When you first open Adobe XD, as with most design apps, you'll see a welcome screen that asks you to either select a ready-made UI kit, or start a new design from scratch (by choosing an artboard). You can also choose to reopen an existing file.

UI Kits

As mentioned in the previous chapter, Adobe XD offers UI kits for Apple iOS, Google Material and Microsoft Windows — these kits contain native UI elements found in the operating system, and you can use them to design quicker mockups rather than recreate these elements yourself. If you were building an iOS app, for example, you could use the Apple iOS kit to extract native design components, such as the status bar or toggle buttons.

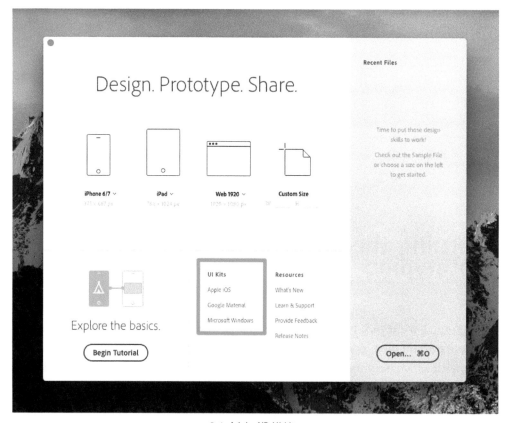

2-1. Adobe XD UI kits

Choosing an Artboard

Over the course of this book we'll be designing a food-ordering iOS app using the standard-size iPhone 7 as a base. So select *iPhone 6/7* from the list of artboards, and let's start prototyping.

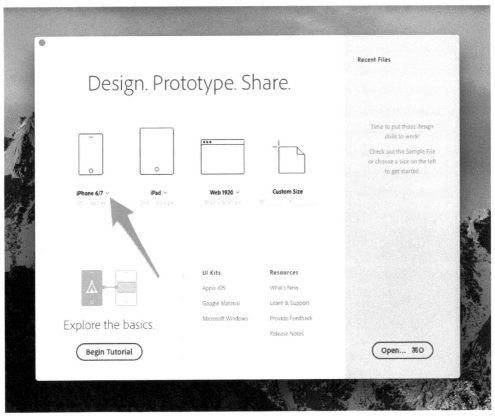

2-2. Choosing an artboard

Returning to an Existing Project

If you already have a design that you've been working on, you can hit **Cmd + O**
(**Ctrl + O** in Windows) to find and open it. Or simply select it from the list of
Recent Files, if you've not long ago opened it.

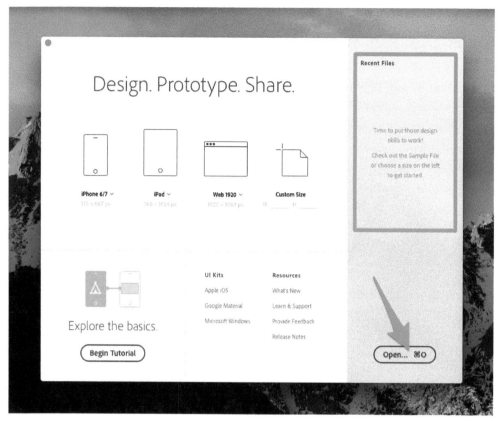

2-3. Opening files

Low-Fidelity Prototyping

Low-fidelity prototyping is about conceptualising ideas in their most basic form — without typography, color or any aesthetics. Why waste time thinking about the visuals when you haven't solidified the layout and the user experience yet?

Our current objective is to use Adobe XD to mock up an idea that you might have already explored with some good old-fashioned pen and paper. After that, when we have our low-fidelity mockup in Adobe XD, we'll use the (rather awesome) prototyping tools to demonstrate user flows (how screens link to other screens), and then ask for feedback.

Over the course of this book, this low-fidelity mockup will evolve into a dynamic, working prototype, then into a high-fidelity prototype with colors, icons, fonts, etc.

Our low-fidelity mockup will be heavily based on Adobe XD's official UI kit, Dishy, which you can download from Adobe[1] if you'd like to take a look now.

Getting Started with Shape Layers

Let's begin with our app's welcome screen. This will consist of the logo, an introductory sentence, and some actionable components such as a navigation bar and search bar.

We'll start by drawing out a few rectangles that will define the basic structure of our screen, where the search function will be the focus. Press **R** to select the Rectangle shape tool.

Now, using the mouse, draw the rectangle until it reaches the full width of the artboard (375px), and 445px in height. You can check these values using the inspector on the right-hand side.

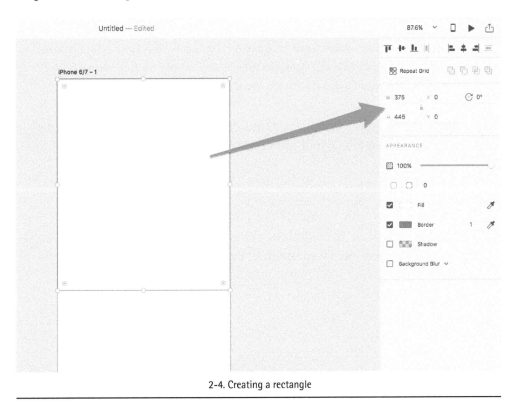

2-4. Creating a rectangle

[1] https://helpx.adobe.com/experience-design/how-to/ux-tips-tricks.html

Snapping Layers to Specific Points

If you begin by hovering your mouse over the top-left corner of the artboard, the mouse will automatically snap to that specific location, and when you drag towards the edges of the canvas, the rectangle edges will snap there too (and other layers, if there are any available). By snapping, Adobe XD is assuming you'll want to align the layer from (or to) that specific location.

Designing With the Inspector

If you found it difficult to create an exact height of 445px (this can be difficult with some mice), use the inspector to declare the height manually by inputting the exact value into the field (the *H* field in this case). You shouldn't encounter any troubles with the width field (*W*) because Adobe XD will have automatically snapped the shape to the artboard edge.

 Using the Arrow Keys

> You can also use the arrows keys to change the values — the ↑ key will increase the value by 1, and the ↓ key will decrease it by 1. If you hold **Shift** while using the arrow keys, the value will increase or decrease by 10 instead of 1.

Now let's create two more rectangles. One will resemble a search field and the other its submit button. Let's start with the submit button.

Create another rectangle, but this time as a 73 x 73px square — hold **Shift** while drawing the shape to maintain aspect ratio.

Drag it so that it snaps to the bottom-right corner of the other rectangle, but first, tap **Esc** to unfocus from the layer and then **Esc** once more to revert back to the move tool.

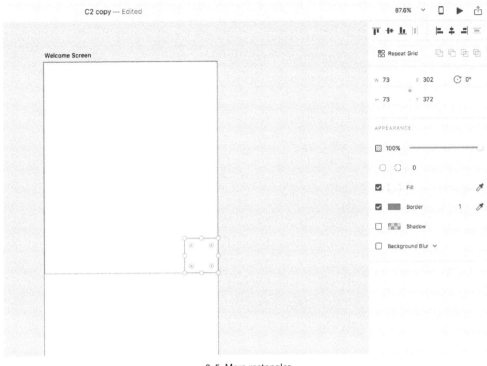

2-5. More rectangles

Repeat this step with another rectangle — 304 x 73px — and drag it to the bottom-left of our original, larger rectangle.

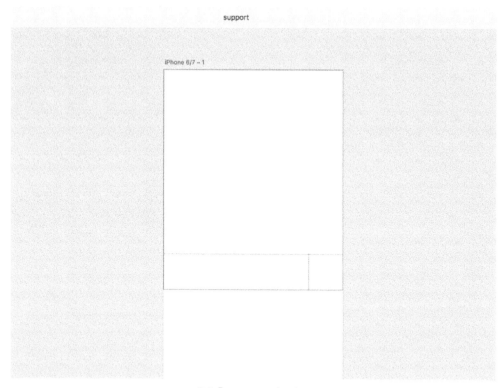

2-6. Even more rectangles

Text Layers

At the moment it's not quite clear what we have here. *We* know that this is a search function, but anybody testing our prototype wouldn't be aware of that, so it's important to add context to low-fidelity mockups. We're going for minimalist, not vague. With that in mind, let's add some text to the input field.

Why You Should Specify Font Sizes Early

When designing low-fidelity screens, you need to be very aware of *space*. Why? Because you can massively overestimate or underestimate the effects of inserting images, defining fonts, and creating styles later down the line (this is the stage we call *high*-fidelity prototyping). It would be devastating to realise that the wonderful lo-fi design we've mocked up, which offers a terrific user experience, doesn't look or respond very well once the visuals have been added.

While low-fidelity mockups are supposed to be basic/minimal, we need to be somewhat realistic with the concept of space. When it comes to drawing shapes I mean the width and height values, but when it comes to text I mean the font size. If you think you'll use a simple sans-serif font in your final design, then stick to a sans-serif system font like Helvetica in your low-fi mockup.

Creating Text Layers

Begin this next step by tapping **T** for Text on the keyboard and clicking on the canvas where you want the text to appear. We want this text layer to be fluid (ie, to resize automatically depending on the text value), so there's no need to *draw* this layer. Fluid text layers have their width and height attributes disabled in the inspector. You have to wrap content manually by adding line breaks using **Return** (**Enter** in Windows).

As for the text value, type "Seafood", since this is a food app.

Keep tapping **Esc** until you revert back to the move tool, and drag-align the text layer towards the left of the input field.

By default, the font should be *Helvetica Neue*, and the weight should be *Regular*, but you should change the font size to *14px* using the inspector. Right now, the color doesn't matter.

Helvetica Neue is a system font that would closely resemble the sans-serif font we'll choose later; 14px is an appropriate font size considering its use. Remember, space and sizing is your focus here, not colors, fonts and other aesthetics.

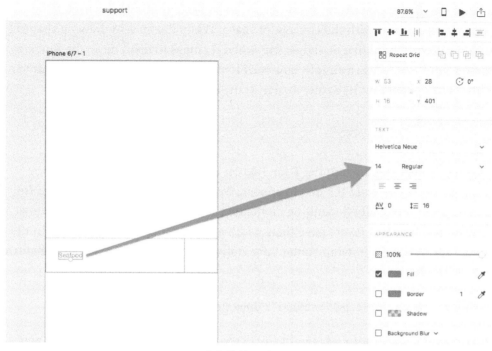

2-7. Fluid text layer

Now let's add some text that describes what the app does, since this is the welcome screen. Press **T** for Text again, but this time draw out the text field using the mouse so we can edit the width and height attributes. We'll estimate the width at 190px and let the text run on for two lines. Make up some lorem ipsum dummy text for the time being. The text will automatically wrap to the second line because we drew out this text layer and defined a width, as opposed to creating a fluid layer.

For now you can insert this text layer anywhere in the lower-third of the screen, but do ensure the font size is 24px — this is the main heading of our screen, so it needs to stand out.

Also, hit the center align button in the inspector.

2-8. Fixed text layer

Duplicating Layers

You can duplicate layers with the keyboard shortcut **Cmd + D** (**Ctrl + D** in Windows), but also by holding **Option** (**Alt** in Windows) and **dragging** the layer, effectively creating a copy. Choose one of the methods and duplicate the main heading text layer, then change the font size of this new text layer to 14px — this will be used as secondary text.

 ### Use the Inspector to Set a Suitable Height

Remember, if you're drawing-out text layers, neither the width *nor* height attributes will be fluid, so make sure your text layers are of a suitable height by using the inspector.

Grouping Layers

Grouping layers allows us to combine layers so they can be moved dependant of one another (or simply because it's cleaner/neater to combine related layers). For example, if we want to move our input field, inclusive of the text layer and the submit button, we can select all the layers at once (**click** each one while holding **Shift**) and use the keyboard shortcut **Cmd + G** (**Ctrl + G** in Windows) to group them together.

You can ungroup layers by selecting the group and hitting **Cmd + Shift + G** (**Ctrl + Shift + G** in Windows).

While we're here, repeat these steps with the text layers that describe what the app does. Grouping should become habitual, as it's a neat way to keep your design organised as it develops.

 Click-Through

> **Double-click** or **Cmd + click** to select layers inside groups — this is known as "click-through".

Smart Guides

Smart Guides were originally introduced in Sketch and later adopted in Photoshop after the feature became a hit. Adobe XD explains them in their help section: *"When you move an object or artboard, use Smart Guides to align the selected object or artboard to other objects or artboards. The alignment is based on the geometry of objects and artboards. Guides appear as the object approaches the edge or center point of other objects."*

Let me start by saying than an object is a common term used to describe a shape layer, text layer, group or bitmap on the canvas. Basically, any type of layer or group is an object.

Guides are visual cues that illustrate how objects align to one another — they can display the distance between two layers, or indicate whether or not a layer has snapped to the bounds of another object or artboard edge. Adobe XD will try to anticipate where you want to move a layer, and automatically snap to that location when you draw close to it, while showing how far you have left until you reach it. You can work out the distance manually by selecting the first layer, holding **Option/Alt,** and hovering over the *second* layer.

Manual Alignments

Let's start by aligning a layer manually, so we understand the difference. A moment ago we grouped two text layers together — select both of them once more (hold **Shift** while you click them) and click the *Align Center (Horizontally)* button in the Inspector, or use the shortcut: **Cmd + Control + C** (**Shift + C** in Windows).

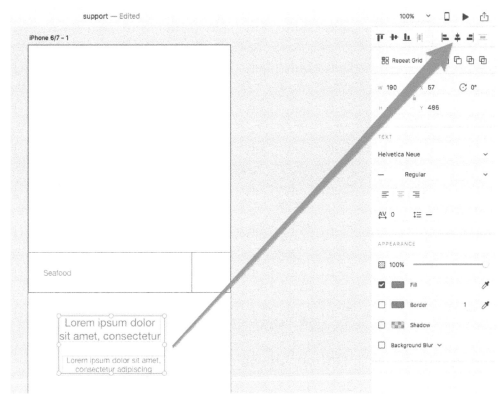

2-9. Manually centering layers

Smart Guides When Moving Layers

Now select the *actual* group. You can either use the *Select* tool (keyboard shortcut: **V**) and select the group by clicking on it, or use the **Esc** key to traverse up to the *parent* container, which is the group. Move it until two things happen:

1. It appears 28px below the form
2. It snaps to the dead-center of the artboard horizontally

You'll know you've done this correctly because the colored lines of the smart guides will illustrate what the object has snapped to (which will be the dead-center of the artboard, as indicated by the vertical line that appears). You'll also notice the relative distance between the search function group and the welcome text group (as indicated by the numerical value).

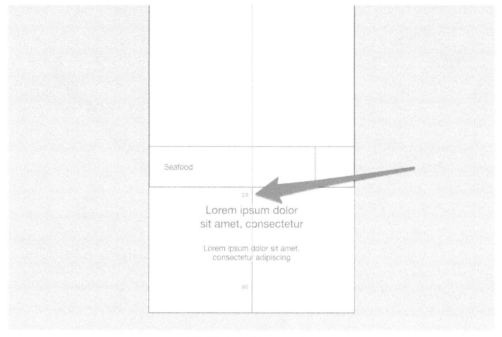

2-10. Aligning with smart guides

Smart Guides With Option/Alt-Hold

Select the bottom-most layer of this group, hold **Option** (**Alt** in Windows), then hover the cursor over the top-most layer. This is a manual approach (also known as **Option/Alt-hold**) to measuring the relative distance between two layers. You can move layers as normal while option-holding, so use the ↑→↓← arrow keys until the distance is 5px.

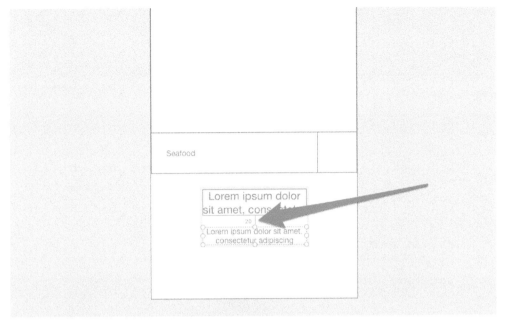

2-11. Guides with option/alt-hold

Let's use what we've learned to add some more elements. So far we've taken our first look at shape layers, text layers, grouping of layers, alignments, smart guides, and some other basics. Let's recap some of that and finish off this screen, starting with a bottom navigation component with four links.

Create a rectangle that's 345 x 44px (44px, width *and* height, is the minimum size for a tap target — tap targets smaller than this are very hard for the user to tap). Use **Option/Alt-Hold** to ensure that the rectangle has a 15px margin on three sides.

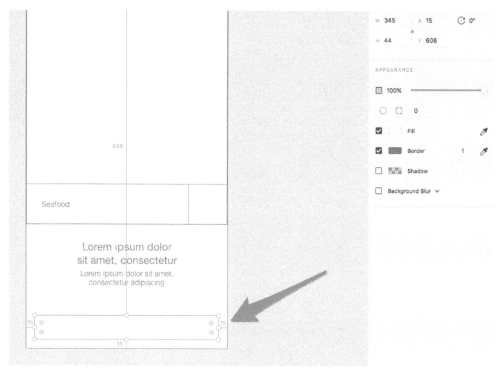

2-12. Recapping smart guides

Now we have the basic shape of the navbar component.

Draw another rectangle where the width is 25% of the navbar's total width (because we'll need to create four links inside the navbar, where each link is 25% of the total width). Start your draw from the top-left corner of the navbar's rectangle. You'll see the smart guides again, indicating that your draw will snap from the corner of that layer, which is what we want.

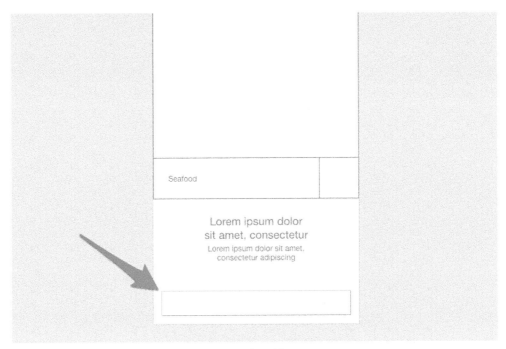

Seafood

Lorem ipsum dolor
sit amet, consectetur

Lorem ipsum dolor sit amet,
consectetur adipiscing

2-13. Drawing with snap

With the Ellipse (**E**) tool, draw a 14 x 14px circle (hold **Shift** to maintain aspect ratio) and group together the navbar link and circle, which substitutes for a navbar icon for the time being. Duplicate this group three times and drag each one horizontally to distribute them evenly inside the navbar.

Finally, **group the entire component**.

2-14. Forming a component

Renaming Layers

We now have a lo-fi mockup of the navbar, but we also have a lot of objects that are named "rectangle" and "group", which is confusing if you're trying to locate a layer within the layer list.

At this moment in time there's no shortcut for renaming layers, so you'll have to double-click on the layer's name in the layer list, and rename it by typing in a new name for the layer. Renaming layers helps you maintain cleanliness in your design, and makes the layer list look a lot less confusing.

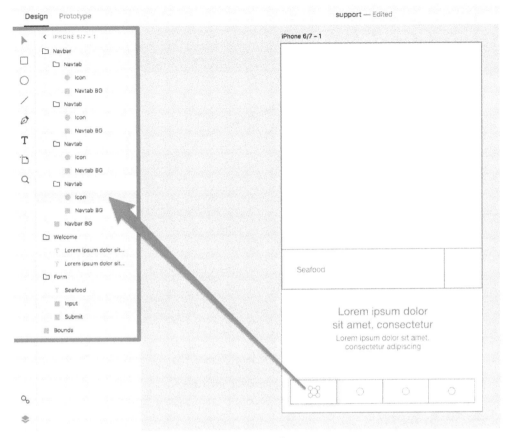

2-15. Renaming layers

Wrap up this screen by creating three more layers:

1. A rectangle, renamed to "Logo BG"
2. A text layer called "DISHY"
3. A group to contain these two layers, renamed to "Logo"

Centralise the group horizontally/vertically in the top space.

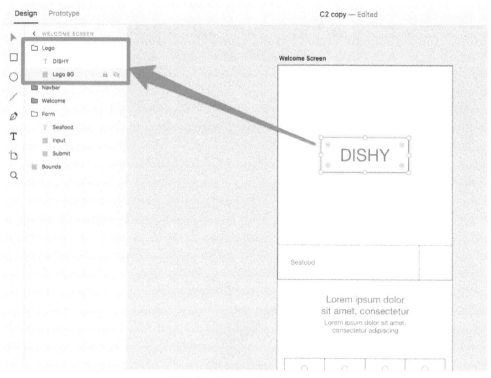

2-16. Wrapping up the first screen

Fast-Forward

Fast-forward 30 minutes and we have an additional screen. When the user has searched for a type of cuisine using the form on the welcome screen, they're then invited to set their location so the app can return results relevant to the user's location.

In the next chapter we'll prototype/demonstrate this user flow, but for now let's finish mocking up this screen while learning about Adobe XD's *other* design tools. From the archive, grab the support file named C2.xd[2] to continue.

---

2. https://github.com/spbooks/jsadobexd1/blob/master/C2.xd

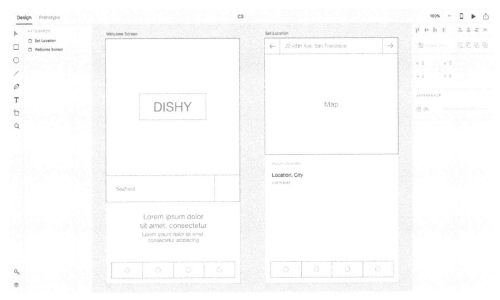

2-17. Fast-forward

Repeat Grids

Repeat grids allow you to repeat objects horizontally and/or vertically — it's a much quicker way of duplicating and distributing objects so you won't have to duplicate and position them manually. Select the "Recent Locations" group from the "Set Location" artboard I've added into the support file, and hit the "Repeat Grid" button in the inspector, or use the keyboard shortcut **Cmd + R (Ctrl + R** in Windows).

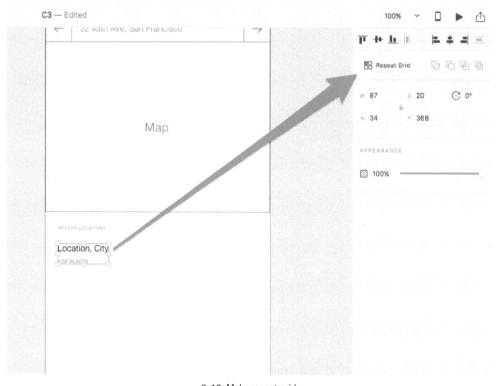

2-18. Make repeat grid

You'll notice that this component now has two tuggable handles. Pull the right one to repeat the component horizontally, and the bottom one to repeat it vertically. In this case, we want to repeat it vertically, so move forward and do that. Note that it doesn't matter if the content overflows the artboard; in fact, in the next chapter we'll learn all about scrollable prototypes.

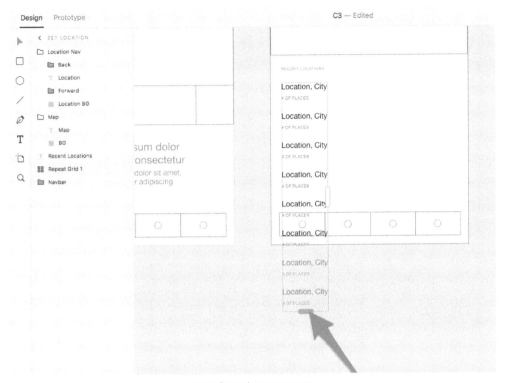

2-19. Repeating components

If you use the cursor to hover over the space in between the repeated objects, you'll be able to click and drag that space to adjust it. Adjust the spacing to 20px (you'll notice the spacing adjustment applies to all repeated objects).

2-20. Adjusting the space between repeated objects

Next: Prototyping User Flows and Receiving Feedback

In the next chapter we'll take a look at the prototyping workspace, where we'll learn how to create user flows and interactions. We'll also learn how to share prototypes, accept comments on them, and even record user flows so we can make video demonstrations of how the prototype works.

Chapter **3**

Prototyping User Flows and Receiving Feedback

Now we have two screens in our design – a welcome screen with a search function, and a location filter screen with a list of recently selected locations. Let's demonstrate how the user would flow from one screen to the other. This is the first time we'll be switching to the "Prototype" workspace, but it won't be the last.

So we have more screens to work with, I've once again added another low-fidelity screen to the design. This is the screen that the user sees after selecting a type of food and a location where they'd like to eat (the *Search Results* screen). I've also downloaded and copied some temporary icons into the mockup (we'll learn about using vectors and iconography in Chapter 6).

Grab the C3.xd[1] file from the archive.

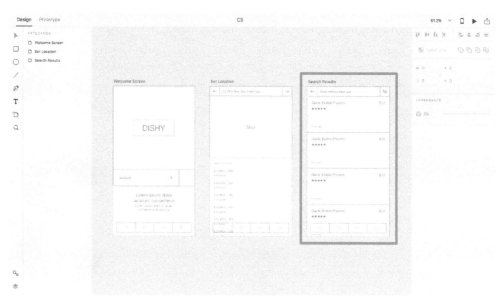

3-1. Added a new screen

Start by switching to the prototype workspace by clicking on the *Prototype* tab in the top-left corner. You can also quickly toggle between the design and prototype workspaces with the keyboard shortcut **Ctrl + Tab (Ctrl + Tab** in Windows).

---

1. https://github.com/spbooks/jsadobexd1/blob/master/C3.xd

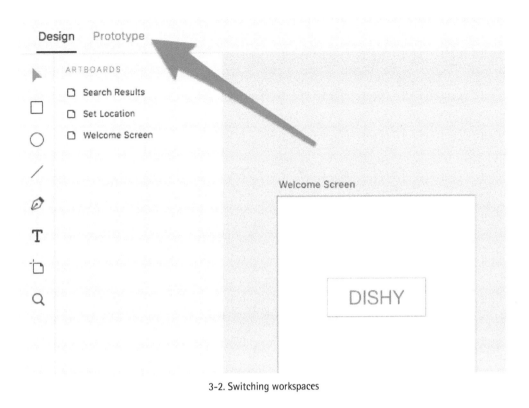

3-2. Switching workspaces

You will now be in the prototype workspace, where the interface and tools available are catered towards prototyping user flows.

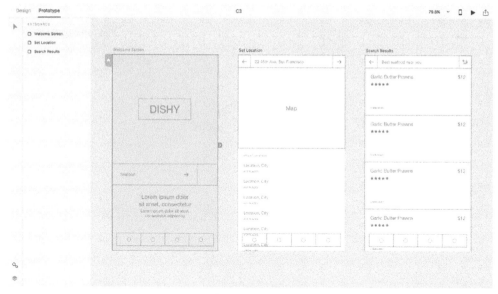

3-3. Prototype workspace

Prototyping Interactions

Let's start by linking the welcome screen to the location filter screen, effectively demonstrating a user flow where the user searches for a type of cuisine, and is then asked to specify *where* they'd like to eat in the location filter screen. Click on the right arrow icon (inside the input field on the welcome screen), where a blue arrow-tab will appear alongside it.

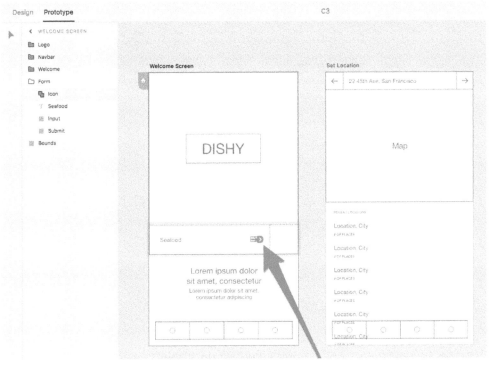

3-4. Creating a user flow

Drag and drop this blue tab into the location filter screen. A user flow will have been created, and a small modal will appear where you can specify transition settings for this user flow – that is, how the screen will transition into the next one (the type of animation effect, the duration of that animation, etc).

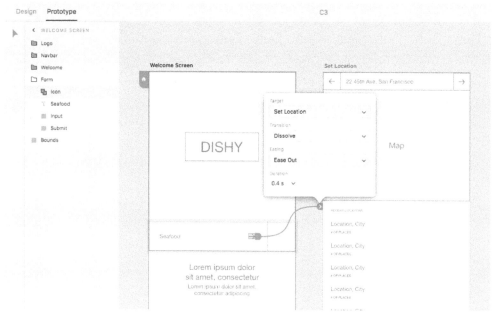

3-5. Flow and transition settings

Later on (when we learn how to preview/test our prototypes), we'll be able to literally click on this icon and be taken to the next screen, as if we were using a real app — this is how we (and our developers, and *maybe* even our clients) use the prototype workspace to test our concept before committing to it.

Next, we'll specify the transition settings for this user flow.

Designing Transitions

Animation comes with its own set of UX challenges. A slow transition can make the user feel like your app is taking too long, whereas a transition that's too fast can leave the user wondering what even happened. And then there's the style of the transition itself. You don't need to do a fade-flip-slide combo to wow the user, a subtle motion is enough to illustrate the result of the user interaction. Let's explore some of the transitions and transition settings that we can use in Adobe XD.

- *Target* (what the screen transitions into):
  - None: Essentially removes the flow
  - Previous Artboard: Returns to previous screen

- [Artboard Name]: Links to another screen
- *Transition* (the visual effect):
  - None: No transition
  - Dissolve: Simple fade transition
  - Slide Left: Slides over from the left
  - Slide Right: Slides over from the right
  - Slide Up: Slides over from the top
  - Slide Down: Slides over from the bottom
  - Push ←/→/↑/↓: Same as slide transition, except the screen sliding in *pushes* the current screen out
- *Easing* (the speed of each interval of the transition):
  - Ease-Out: Transition will start at full speed/finish slowly
  - Ease-In: Transition will start slowly/finish at full speed
  - Ease-In-Out: Start slow, full-speed at middle, finish slow
  - None: The transition will not accelerate/decelerate (linear)
- *Duration*: Overall time it takes for the transition to complete

 Using Transitions

Page transitions are less common on websites, therefore a *None* transition is quite normal for website prototypes. Some web-*apps* on the other hand *do* support transitions, which is why the transition options are nonetheless available in all cases.

For further reading on easings (notably, the different types of easings and their effect on user experience), check out my article on micro-interactions and easings on SitePoint[2].

Because we linked the welcome screen to the set location screen, the *Target* setting has already been defined. *Slide Left* is a suitable option for the *Transition* setting because it creates motion (the destination screen slides in from the right, implying that it was the next screen in a series of screens — this is the default setting on iOS and some areas of Android).

Ease-out is a suitable easing for this user flow because it forces the animation to be faster at the beginning, creating a seemingly swift transition that doesn't delay

---

[2.] https://www.sitepoint.com/animations-using-easings-to-craft-smarter-interactions/

the user too much, then gracefully slows down so the user has a little extra time to understand what's happened. In most cases, the default *Duration* setting of 0.4 seconds is more than optimal.

Let's roll with these settings.

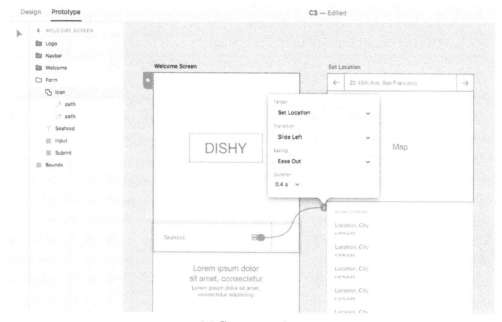

3-6. First screen settings

From the *Set Location* screen, create a user flow back to the *Welcome Screen*. Select *Previous Artboard* as the *Target*, which will automatically reverse the transition last used. For example, if you used *Slide Left* to enter the screen, *Slide Right* will be used as you return to the previous screen.

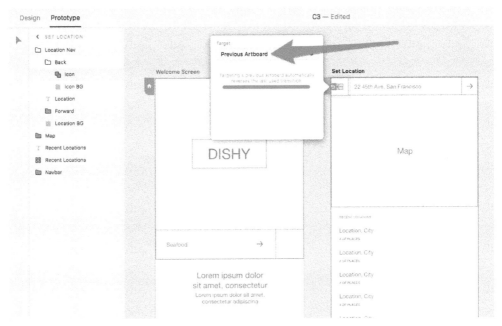

3-7. Previous artboard settings

Repeat these steps, linking *Set Location* to *Search Results*.

3-8. Linking a second screen

And vice-versa.

3-9. And vice-versa

At any moment you can click on an artboard to see an overview of which screens link to it, and which screens it links to. Prototyping is wonderfully visual in Adobe XD!

While apps like Marvel, Framer, Origami and InVision are certainly more *powerful* when it comes to prototyping (functionality like fixed elements, dynamic input fields and embeddable web content has existed in these apps for a while now), Adobe XD releases feature updates on a monthly basis. It's catching up fast, and each version is reasonably stable.

Besides that, Adobe XD offers something that no other design app does: a unified design + prototyping experience. XD is not a companion to a design app like Photoshop or Sketch, it *is* the design app, *and* the prototyping app. Being able to seamlessly switch between the *Design* and *Prototype* workspaces makes designing and prototyping with Adobe XD silky smooth.

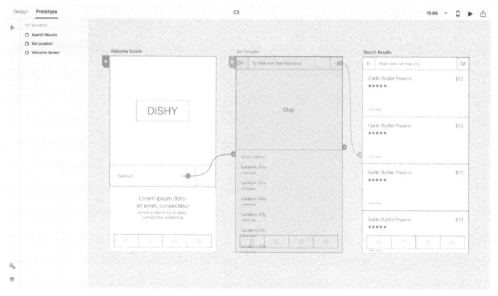

3-10. A user flow overview

Previewing Prototypes

Shall we try it out?

Desktop Preview

Hit the *Desktop Preview* icon.

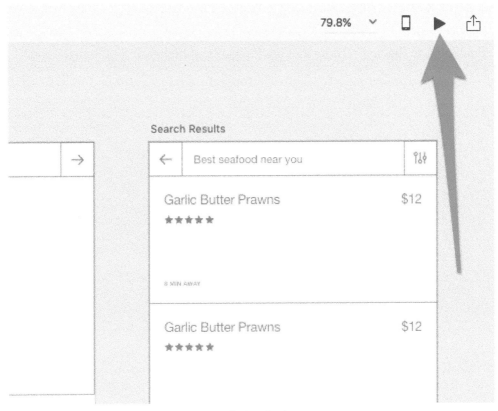

3-11. Desktop Preview

Desktop Preview is an opportunity for *you* to test the prototype before you hastily send it off to others for feedback. Click on the hotspots we defined earlier to navigate the prototype. Is there anything we've overlooked? Hint: there is.

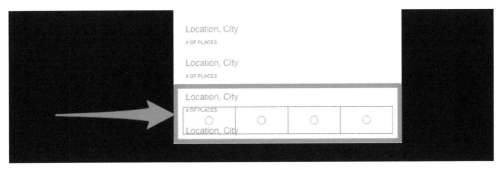

3-12. Ah, there's a mistake

Firstly, in the *Set Location* screen, the navigation is drowning under the content. It needs to be on top, so switch back to the *Design* workspace and reorder the component in the layer list by moving (dragging) it higher up in the hierarchy.

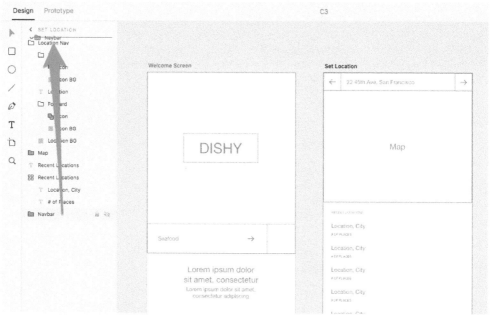

3-13. Fixed

Creating Scrollable Prototypes

Secondly, we have overflowing content in *Search Results*. However, we can't scroll down to view this content when previewing the prototype in Desktop Preview mode. We can fix this by selecting the artboard in the *Design* workspace and resizing it until it holds all of the content in artboard.

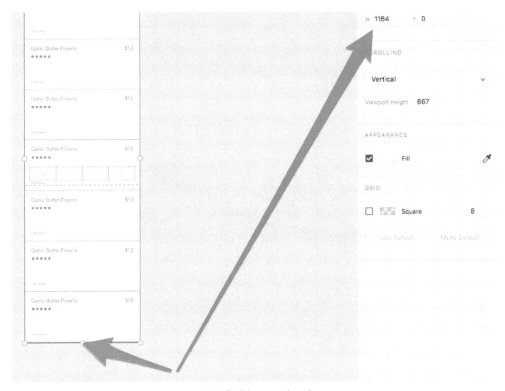

3-14. Resizing an artboard

Will this undesirably make the screen longer in Desktop Preview mode? No, because the viewport height is still 667px – this is the height in which you view the prototype (as indicated by the dashed blue line in *Design* mode) versus its total height.

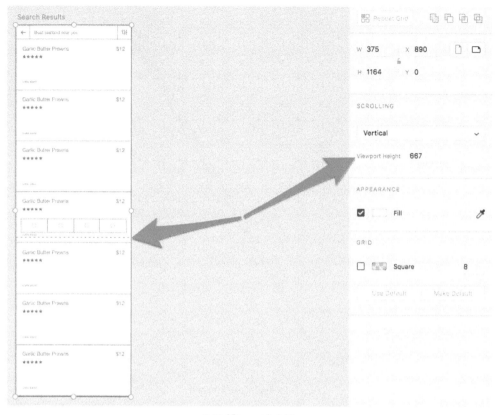

3-15. Viewport height

Now you can scroll the prototype in Desktop Preview mode.

 Creating Sticky Elements

Even though you can scroll prototypes, we cannot (yet) create sticky elements like fixed headers and footers, hence why the navigation component floats awkwardly in place (it doesn't remain on the screen while you scroll). Adobe have assured me this is a feature they're working on right now.

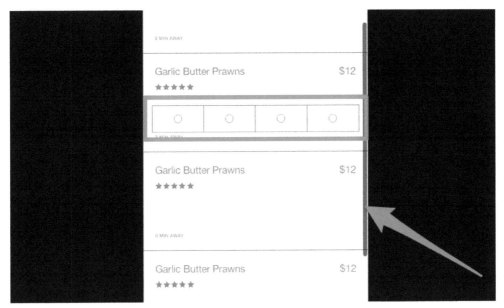

3-16. Scrolling prototypes

Device Preview

Now that we've ironed out the creases, let's test our prototype on a real device. Desktop Preview is fine for first-round testing, but this is a mobile app that's intended to be navigated with fingers and thumbs, not mice and touchpads.

Start by downloading the Adobe Experience Design app for iOS from the iTunes store[3], which is free.

 What About Android?

> For designs intended for Android, there is an Android-equivalent app available from the Play store[4].

When you've installed the app on your device, hit the *Device Preview* button to begin. As the instructions say, connect your iOS or Android device to your computer using the USB cable.

---

[3]. https://itunes.apple.com/us/app/adobe-experience-design-preview/id1146597773

[4]. https://play.google.com/store/apps/details?id=com.adobe.sparklerandroid

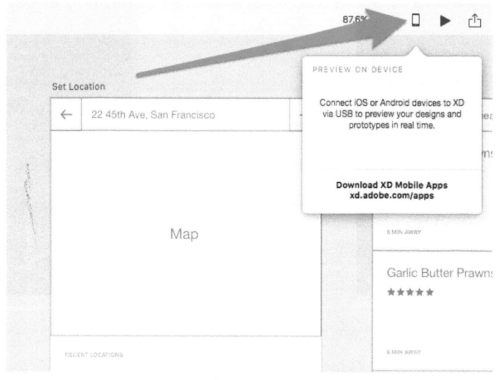

3-17. Connecting to a device

Ensure you have your document open on the desktop when you connect, or, alternatively, load the file from Creative Cloud from within the Adobe XD app (you'll need to ensure the file exists in the Creative Cloud folder on your computer).

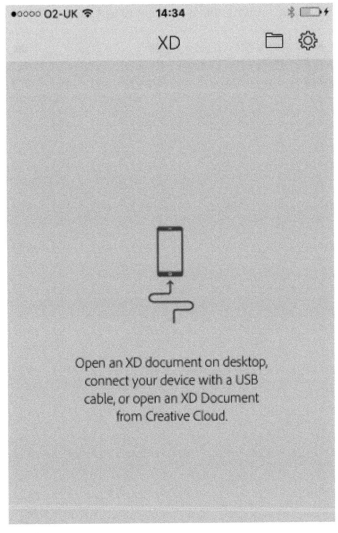

3-18. Loading a file via Creative Cloud

 ## No Internet Access?

If you don't have internet access, but you've loaded a prototype previously, Adobe XD for iOS or Android will automatically load the last version cached by the app. Either way, you must be connected via the USB cable at all times.

When you're all set up, simply select a screen to test it.

3-19. Selecting a screen to test

Device Preview is pretty straightforward. However, one feature that's easy to miss is the ability to disable hotspot hints. You should disable hints when you need to figure out if a call-to-action is obvious enough, and enable them at any other time.

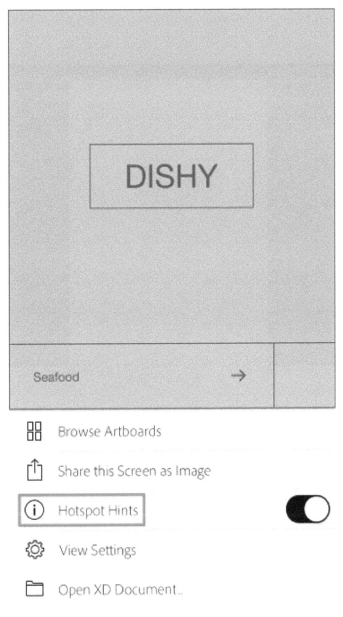

3-20. Disabling hotspot hints

Recording Your Tests

Another noteworthy feature is the ability to record a screencast where you demonstrate the prototype. This is a useful way to quickly showcase prototypes to teammates or clients. While in Desktop Preview mode, simply hit the record button, although be aware that you can't record user flows in a maximised window.

3-21. Recording user flows

When you close the window, select an export location from the file chooser modal to export the recording as a .mov file.

Sharing Prototypes and Gathering Feedback

Now let's open ourselves up to feedback. Begin by clicking the *Share Online* button and giving this prototype a name. You can optionally uncheck the *Allow Comments* box to disable comments, but for now let's allow comments. Click *New Link* to continue.

3-22. Sharing prototypes online

 Sharing Shortcuts

You can also use the **Cmd + Shift + E** shortcut (**Ctrl + Shift + E** on Windows) to begin sharing online.

Press the *Copy Link* button to copy a shareable URL to the clipboard, then hand it out to your teammates.

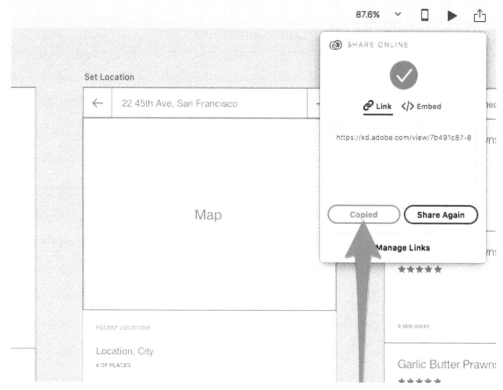

3-23. Creating share links

Paste the copied URL into the browser.

Pretty straightforward stuff. From this shared webpage you can:

- See when the prototype was last updated
- Interact with the prototype from a user perspective
- Cycle through screens using the left, right and home buttons

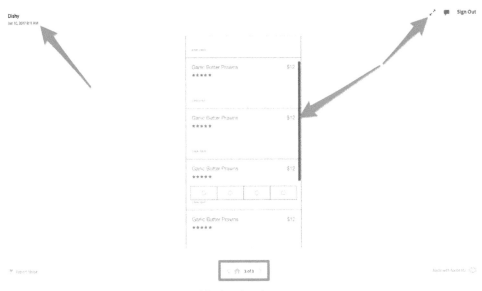

3-24. Viewing shared prototypes

And finally, make comments — this is where the feedback happens.

First, click on the comment icon, then use the comment box to start a conversation. So that comments remain contextual, conversations are unique to each artboard (ie, if you switch to another screen, only comments for that screen will show).

Click *Reply* to respond to a comment.

3-25. Making comments

To ensure it's crystal clear what you're referring to in your comment, you can drop a numbered pin onto the artboard. Your comment will then be associated with that number. Click the *Pin to Artboard* button, then click on the artboard to drop the pin.

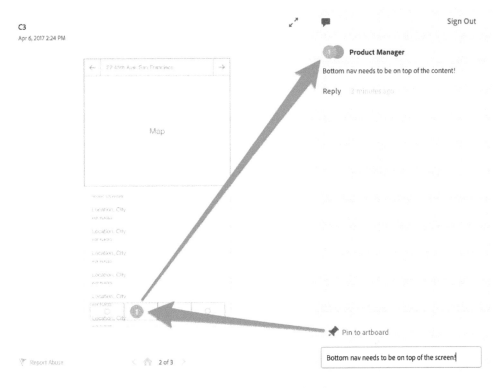

3-26. Pinning comments to artboard

If you click *Share Again*, then *New Link* from the *Share Online* modal (in the prototype workspace), teammates can view an updated version of your prototype with an empty, refreshed comments section. Comments are unique to the share link on which they were made. Don't worry, creating new share links won't erase the existence of the older links — they'll still work.

 Share Links Don't Update Automatically

Share links **do not** automatically sync to the current state of your design. If you have changes to show off, you must create a new share link and share it with your teammates.

Next: Getting Visual with the Property Inspector

In the next chapter we'll start to tackle the visual design of our app by defining colors, fonts and text styles. Well learn about the property inspector's primary use (it's ability to style layers), and we'll learn about each of the styles, how to apply them, and how to customise them. We'll then wrap up the chapter by applying some of those styles to our design.

Chapter

4

Getting Visual with the Property Inspector

In this chapter we'll learn about the property inspector, adding styles to our low-fidelity prototype as we transition our design into a high-fidelity mockup with colors, fonts and images. We'll start by learning about all the styles available to us, as well as how to customise them. Then we'll work on our design using those styles.

Let's bring our design to life!

Styling Layers with the Property Inspector

We were briefly introduced to the inspector in the first chapter of this book. And in the second and third chapters, we touched on some of its features (artboard selection, vertical scrolling, layer alignment and repositioning, etc). Now we'll learn about its other uses, ie, its ability to style layers.

Let's run through the various styling options available (what they do, how to customise them, etc) before we continue with the walkthrough. For now, you can simply sit back and read.

Dimensions and Offsets

- *W*: defines the width of an object
- *H*: defines the height of an object

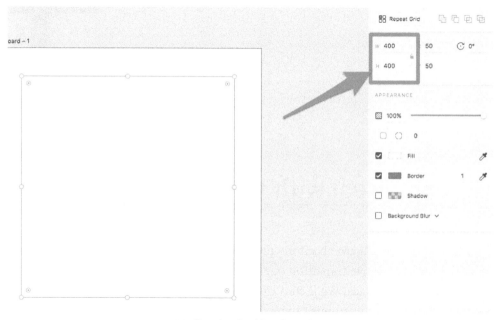

4-1. Changing the object dimensions

- *X*: defines the distance from the left-side of the artboard
- *Y*: defines the distance from the top of the artboard

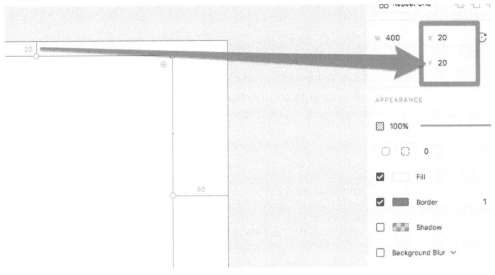

4-2. Changing the object's offset

🔲 *Rotation*: specifies the angle of rotation in degrees (°)

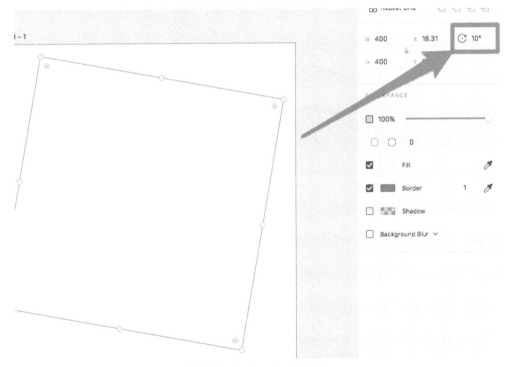

4-3. Changing the object rotation

Opacity

Opacity defines how transparent an object is, and is the first styling option under the *Appearance* heading. Adjust the slider to choose a value between 0% and 100%, or use the number keys (**1-9**) to define a value manually. Here are a few examples:

- **1**: 10%
- **3**: 30%
- **1**, then **3** in rapid succession: 13%
- **0**: 100% (opaque)
- **0**, then **0** in rapid succession: 0% (invisible)

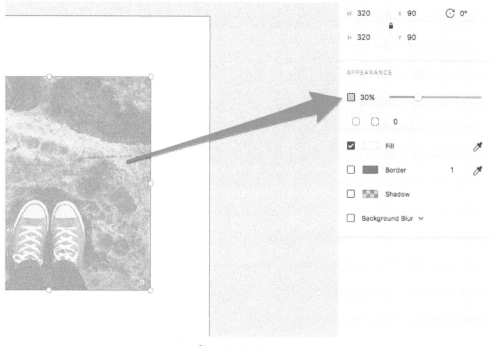

4-4. Changing the object opacity

Corner Radius

Corner Radius defines the roundness of corners on rectangle shape layers. By default, the *Same radius for all corners* button is selected, and the default value is

0. If you had a rectangle shape layer and changed this value to *100*, each corner of the rectangle would be rounded by a value of 100px.

 Check the Tooltips

> Not every styling option has a label describing what that option does. If you're not sure, and you don't want to refer to this book, hover over the button/option with the cursor to reveal the descriptive tooltip.

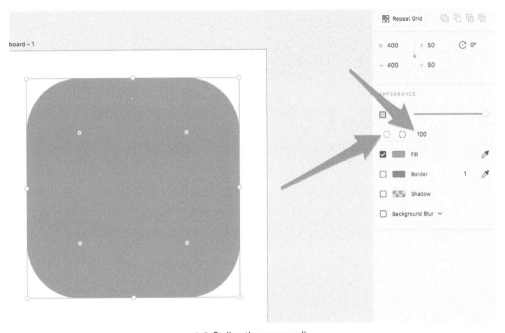

4-5. Styling the corner radius

Different radius for each corner (hover over the buttons to reveal the tooltips, if you're not sure) will allow the corner radius to take four values instead of one — one value for each corner in clockwise order: top-left, top-right, bottom-right, bottom-left.

50, 50, 0, 50, for instance, would create a corner radius of 50px on each corner of the rectangle, except the bottom-right one.

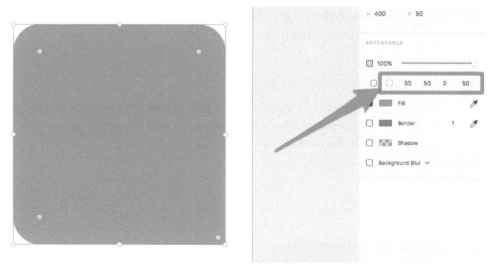

4-6. Styling complex corner radii

Fill

Fill is used to determine the color of a text/shape layer. Click on the rectangular color sample (next to the *Fill* label in the inspector) to reveal the color picker, where you can then specify a color value for the currently selected layer.

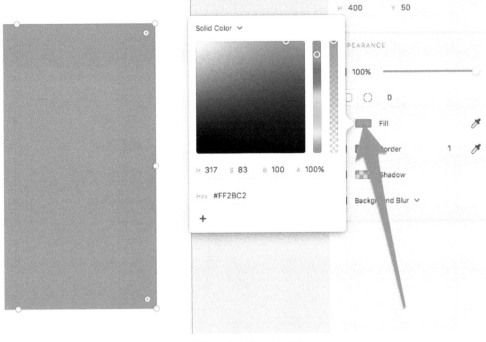

4-7. Revealing the color picker

Color Format

Adobe XD supports *HSBA* (**H**ue, **S**aturation, **B**rightness, **A**lpha) or *Hex* color formats.

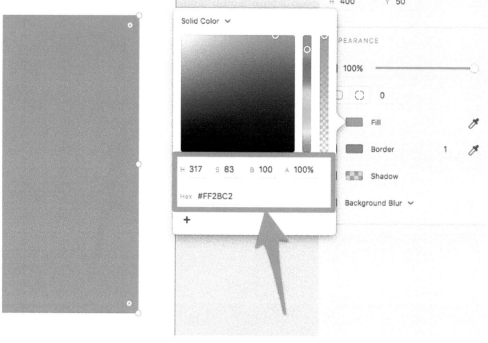

4-8. Color formats

Color Palette

If you click on the large square block on the left of the color picker, you'll be able to roughly change the saturation and brightness of the chosen color. And with the slider that follows (slightly to the right), you'll be able to change the color itself (the hue). With the final slider (on the far-right), you'll be able to change the alpha-transparency of the color — this value will only be reflected in the HSBA format.

As you interact with this color palette, the *HSBA* and *Hex* values will update accordingly to reflect your chosen color.

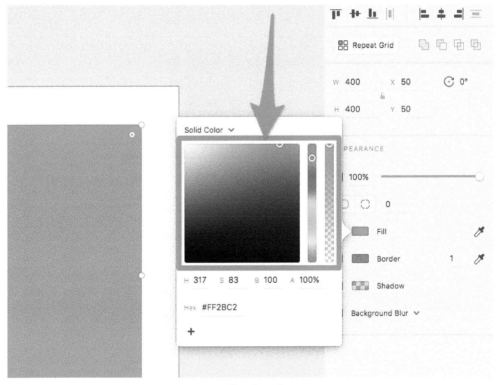

4-9. Choosing colors

Document Colors

Finally, at the very bottom of the color picker, there is a + icon that lets you add the chosen color to your curated collection of commonly used document colors. If there are any colors you'll use multiple times (there probably will be), save them by clicking on the + icon. All saved colors will appear right alongside the + icon.

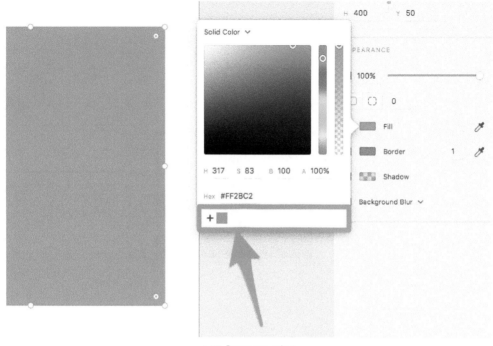

4-10. Document colors

Gradients

In the very top-left corner of the color picker there is a select box (it will say *Solid Color* by default) that allows you to select an alternative type of fill – a *Gradient*. When you select this option, another slider (with two non-adjustable handles at both ends) will be added to the color picker. You can select and then define a different color for each handle, and have the fill fade from one color to the next.

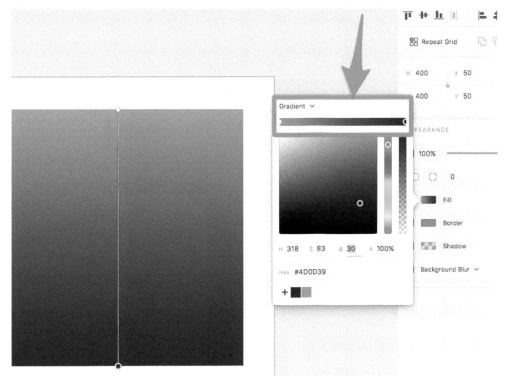

4-11. Gradients

Even though these handles are non-adjustable in the color picker interface, you can move them around on the canvas to change the direction of the color fade effect.

4-12. Changing the fade direction

If you click anywhere on the slider between the two handles (either on the canvas, or on the color picker), you can add an additional handle. This handle can add an extra color to the gradient, helping you create complex color fade effects.

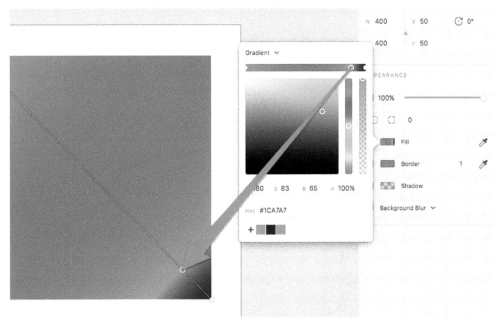

4-13. Creating complex fade effects

Eyedropper Tool

If you want to reuse a color that already exists in the design, but you didn't save it to your colors collection, you can select the *Eyedropper* tool (which appears to the right of the *Fill* label) and define a color by clicking on the canvas. A magnifying glass will replace the mouse cursor to help you extract the desired color accurately.

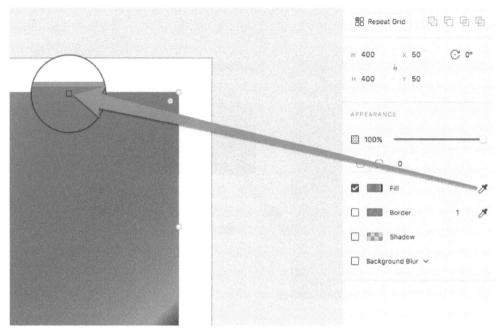

4-14. Extracting with the eyedropper

Border

Border uses all the same options as *Fill*, except it allows for an extra numerical value, which is the width of the border. Right now there are no other options available (such as a dashed border) – only a solid border.

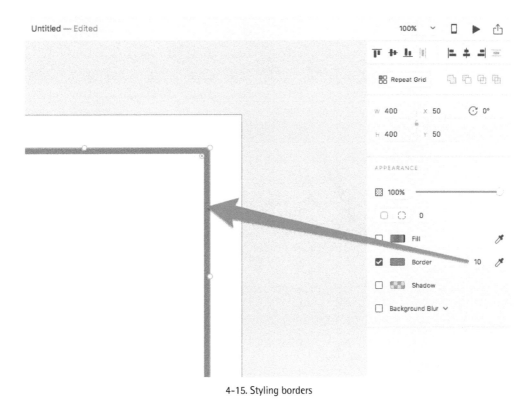

4-15. Styling borders

Shadow

Shadow is the same as *Fill*, but accepts an *X*, *Y* and *B* value (left offset, top offset, and blur, respectively).

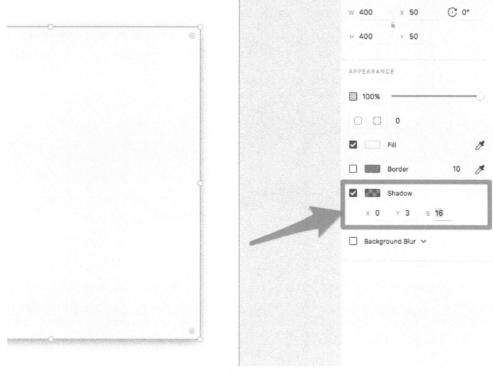

4-16. Styling shadows

Background Blur

Background Blur changes the visibility of the content underneath the currently selected layer (this is useful for creating semi-transparent modal dialogues, for example).

- *Blur Amount*: how blurry the content underneath will appear
- *Brightness*: how light/dark the content underneath will appear
- *Effect Opacity*: how eminent the background blur will appear (a value of 100% would ensure the effect would not be seen)

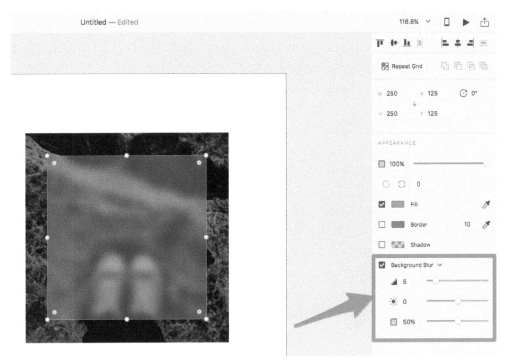

4-17. Creating background blurs

Object Blur

From the select box (where the current/default option is *Background Blur*), there is another option: *Object Blur*. *Object Blur* only has one value, the *Blur Amount* – how much the currently selected object will blur around the edges (you'd probably only use this as a fancy visual effect).

Object Blur blurs the actual object, whereas *Background Blur* acts as a filter on top of a background image.

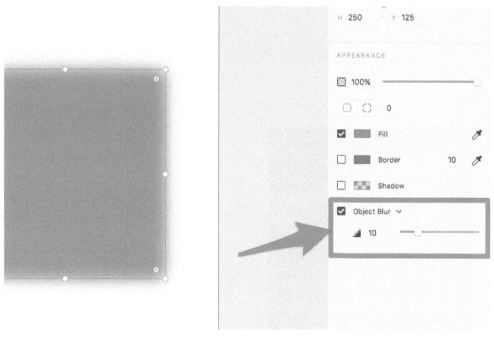

4-18. Creating object blurs

Hiding Styles

Fill, *Border*, *Shadow* and *Background Blur* styles can be switched off by deselecting their respective checkboxes.

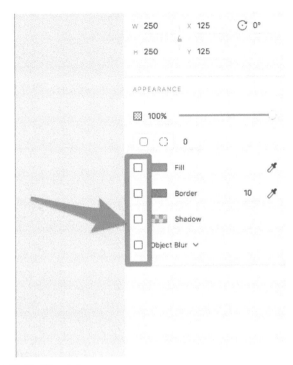

4-19. Disabling styles

Font Styles (*for text layers only*)

We already familiarised ourselves (briefly) with text styles when we were designing our low-fidelity mockup in chapter two. But for the sake of completeness, let's briefly recap:

- *Font*: defines the font of the text layer
- *Font Size*: defines the font size (in px) of the text layer
- *Font Weight*: defines the font weight of the text layer
    - Bold: **Cmd + B (Ctrl + B** in Windows)
    - Italic: **Cmd + I (Ctrl + I** in Windows)
    - Other weights: you'll have to select them manually
- *Left/Center/Right Align*: aligns the text inside the text layer
- *Character Spacing*: the space (in px) between each character
- *Line Spacing*: the space (in px) between each line

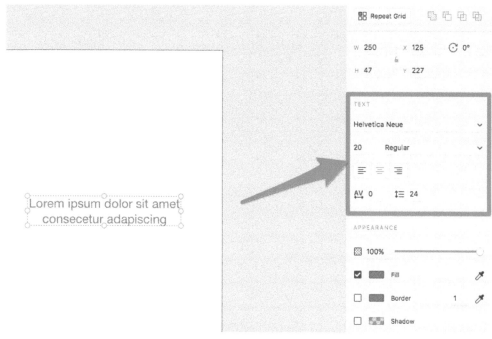

4-20. Styling text layers

Quick Exercise: Styling Layers

Now we know what each style does, let's begin styling the layers in our design. We won't use every style mentioned in the overview above, but we will use the important ones at least.

Let's start with the welcome screen.

Styling the Welcome Text

Select the largest text layer in the lowest third of the screen (this will be the heading of the welcome text). Currently, it uses "lorem ipsum" as dummy text. Press **Return** to enter editing mode, and type "Make ordering in the new going out".

Press **Esc** to exit editing mode.

4-21. Styling the heading layer

Now change the font size to 24px. Naturally, this will make the text layer larger, so we'll need to rearrange the text layer underneath so there is still a 5px space between the two layers. Switch to the text layer underneath and rearrange it (the smart guides will help you while moving the layer).

4-22. Rearranging the layers

Finally, switch back to the heading layer and change the fill color to **#DF0000** (a reddish color). Add this color to the document colors collection by clicking the **+** icon.

4-23. Coloring the heading layer

Repeat these steps with the text layer underneath, changing the color to **#7C7E81** and adding it to the document colors.

Styling the Form Button

Now let's style the form button.

Select the smallest rectangle in the form component (the rectangle on the far right). Apply the following styles:

- *W*: 44
- *H*: 44
- *Corner Radius*: 44
- *Fill*: the red color from our saved document colors
- *Border*: uncheck

4-24. SStyling the form butto

Rearrange this layer until there is a 15px space between the layer and the right-side of the artboard, and a 15px space between the layer and the bottom of the form component.

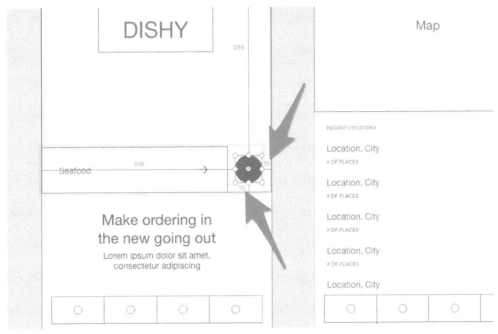

4-25. Rearranging the form button

Styling the Background

Now let's add a background image to the design.

You should have noticed by now that there is an image in the *Pasteboard* artboard (if you don't remember from way back in the first chapter, any layers that are not inside an artboard will automatically reside in the *Pasteboard* artboard).

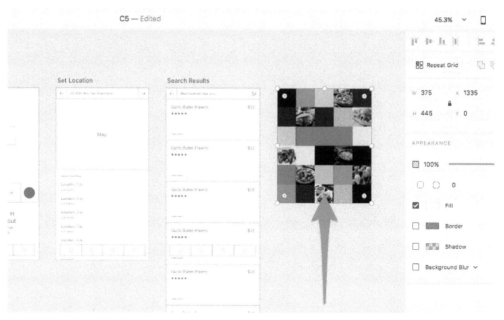

4-26. Locating the image

Drag this image over to the *Welcome Screen* artboard.

4-27. Dragging the image

In the layer list, drag this layer much further down the hierarchy until it rests above the *Bounds* layer (because right now the image is hiding all of our wonderful content).

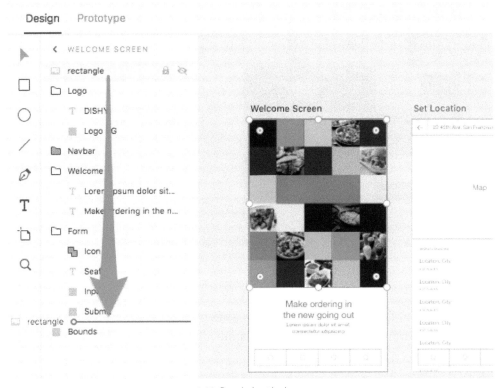

4-28. Reordering the layers

Styling the Input Field

Now, when we style the input field in the form component, it won't disappear into the white background of the screen. Select the input field, then add the following styles:

- *W*: 270
- *H*: 44
- *Corner Radius*: 22
- *Border*: uncheck

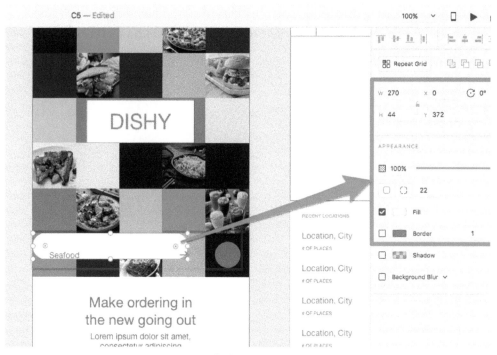

4-29. Styling the input field

Move the input field layer with the **arrow keys** by 15px towards the bottom-right corner of the artboard, so the layer looks more aligned with the red, circular button.

4-30. Moving the input field

 Tidying Up

Move the "Seafood" text layer and the right-arrow icon inwards, about 7px, so the spacing of these layers looks a little more adjusted to the newly resized input field layer.

Styling the Logo

Let's quickly adjust the logo, too.

Select the *Logo BG* layer and delete it with the **Delete** key (**Backspace** on Windows). Make the text layer white (#FFFFFF).

4-31. Designing the logo

Styling the Menu

Let's move onto the *Set Location* screen now, more specifically the topmost menu component. Select the background layer of the back button (*Icon BG*) and apply the following styles:

- *Border*: uncheck
- *Fill*: #59D0B6 (click the + icon in the color picker to add it to the document colors, as we'll use this color again)

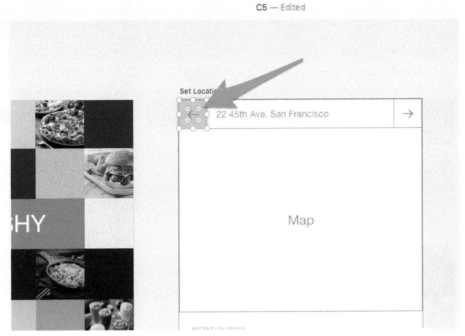

4-32. Styling the back button

Select the background layer of the overall menu component (*Location BG*) and apply the following styles:

- *Fill*: #EE1528 (add to document colors)
- *Border*: uncheck

4-33. Styling the menu background

Select the background layer of the forward icon this time:

- *Fill*: #DF0000 (already in document colors)
- *Border*: uncheck

4-34. Styling the forward button

Finally, make any icons and text in this menu component white (#FFFFFF), then repeat all these styles with the menu component on the third screen (*Search Results*), so they are identical, apart from their text content.

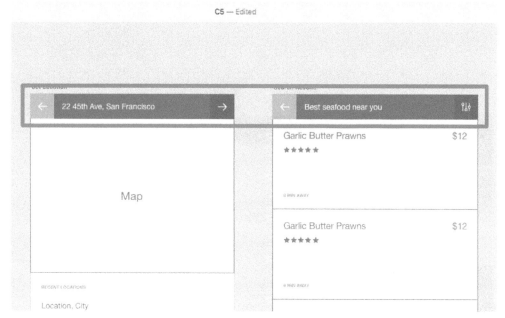

4-35. Styling the menu colors

Next: Hi-Fi Prototyping with Symbols and Repeat Grids

In the next chapter, we'll explore some of the more complex aspects of styling layers. We'll learn about maintaining visual consistency with symbols, as well as how to import real content into our design, while taking a deeper look at repeat grids. We'll also add some imagery and learn about masking.

Chapter **5**

Hi-Fi Prototyping With Symbols and Repeat Grids

In this chapter, we'll learn two features that are designed to help you maintain visual consistency (and save you countless hours!) when high-fidelity prototyping. These are – how to create and use symbols, and how to automate the process of adding styles and content to components inside repeat grids.

High-fidelity prototyping is the act of taking a validated and improved low-fidelity mockup and adding visual styles to it — we'll use symbols and repeat grids to speed up this process. By the end of this chapter we'll have a fully-styled design, minus some icons (which we'll tackle in the following chapter).

First, we'll discuss why maintaining visual consistency is important, and how symbols can help us achieve that.

Maintaining Visual Consistency With Symbols

When styles aren't consistent in a design, the user finds it hard to learn how to use the interface, and quickly becomes frustrated. When styles *are* consistent, the user learns:

- What certain colors represent (eg, red = error)
- What certain font sizes mean (eg, largest size = a heading)
- How to advance to the next stage (eg, right-aligned buttons)

A lack of visual consistency is confusing and jarring for the user, and more styles means more code, which results in:

1. More work for the developer/development team
2. A bulkier codebase, which can make the app/website slower

Symbols can help us maintain visual consistency.

What Are Symbols?

Symbols help you reuse commonly used design components over and over again, while keeping each instance of that design component visually consistent. Imagine a search icon that appears on every screen (or at least most of them) in the design. Now imagine that you notice something wrong with it. If you had turned this search icon into a symbol, you would only need to edit one instance of the search icon for the changes to reflect on every other search icon that appears in the design. It saves you crucial amounts of time at crucial moments, and also gives you the peace of mind that your designs are visually consistent.

Without symbols, you'd have to locate and edit every single instance of that search icon manually. I'll leave you to wonder how much time editing that search icon alone could take up!

Our bottom nav component, which appears on every screen, is a terrific example of a design component that could be used as a symbol. Let's create a symbol from this component and reuse it.

Creating Symbols

Start by selecting the bottom nav component, then switching from the layer list to the symbols list by clicking on the symbols icon at the very bottom of the toolbar. Alternatively, you can use the keyboard shortcut **Cmd + Shift + Y** (a keyboard shortcut for Windows has not been implemented yet).

 Getting Back to the Layer List

Hit **Cmd + Y** (Mac only) to switch back to the layer list.

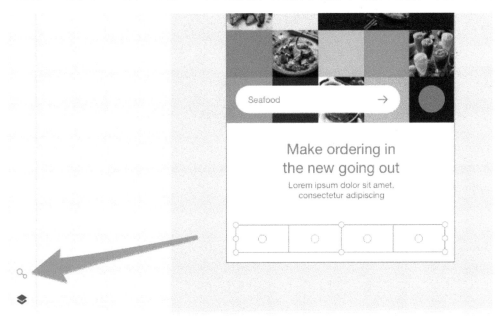

5-1. Switching to the symbols list

Now let's convert the bottom nav component to a symbol by clicking the + icon in the symbols list, or by using the shortcut **Cmd + K** (again, no shortcut for Windows yet).

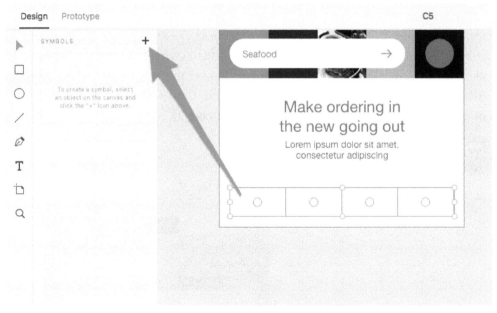

5-2. Creating a symbol

Our bottom nav component is now one instance of a symbol (until we create more instances, that is), and you'll also notice that a reference to the symbol now appears in the symbols list.

5-3. Our first symbol

Inserting Symbols

If we made visual changes to the bottom nav component at this stage, those changes would **not** be reflected in the bottom nav components on *other* screens. This is because we haven't explicitly confirmed they are instances of the symbol we created moments ago, so we need to delete these components from the canvas, and re-add them as linked instances.

If you think that sounds inconvenient, it's because it is. To avoid this inconvenience you should convert commonly used elements to symbols *as you design* the first instance.

Let's learn how to add and remove instances:

Start by selecting all the bottom nav components (not the one used to create the symbol!) while holding **Shift**, then tapping **Delete** (**Backspace** in Windows) to delete them.

Now drag our symbol from the symbol list to the exact spots where the bottom nav components previously existed.

5-4. Creating instances of symbols

Great, now all of these symbol instances are linked.

 Color Hints

Symbols are outlined in green when selected — this is to indicate/remind us that styling the current object has ramifications for all other instances of this symbol.

Editing Instances

Now that all instances of the bottom nav component are linked to the symbol, let's style this component. We already know how to style layers, so this step should be a total breeze.

 You Can Edit Any Symbol Instance

It doesn't matter which instance you make changes to, since they are all linked together by a symbol. If you edit one instance of a symbol, all other instances of that symbol will follow suit.

Navigate to the *Navbar BG* layer, either by clicking through to it on the canvas, or by selecting it from the layer list.

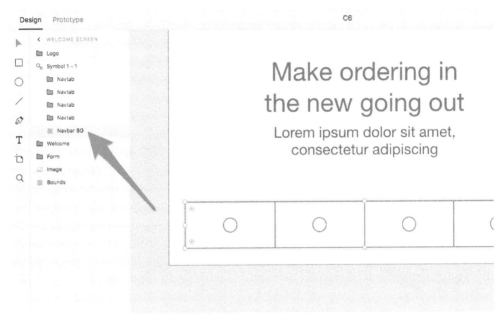

5-5. Selecting the navbar background

Add a *Fill* of **#F6F6F6**, a *Corner Radius* of **44px** (this is equal to the value of the height, which is also 44px), and remove the border by unchecking it. While you're here, I'd also recommend adding this color to the document colors.

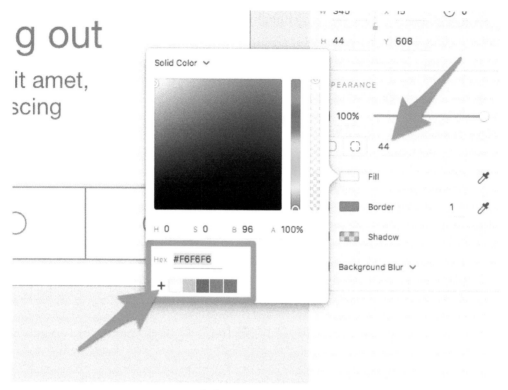

5-6. Styling the navbar background

You **won't** notice any changes yet — this is because, higher up in the layer hierarchy, each *Navtab* has a rectangle background that blocks the view of the main *Navbar* background.

If you remember, we created these rectangle shapes (one for each navtab) back in chapter two, to illustrate that all navtabs should have the same overall width, regardless of how wide each icon inside the navtab is. This allows us to align the future navbar icons within these rectangles, and ultimately distribute them evenly across the navbar component, with complete accuracy.

Since we still require these bounds, we shouldn't delete them; instead, we can hide their *Fill* and *Border* styles (smart guides will still work even if we can't see these layers!).

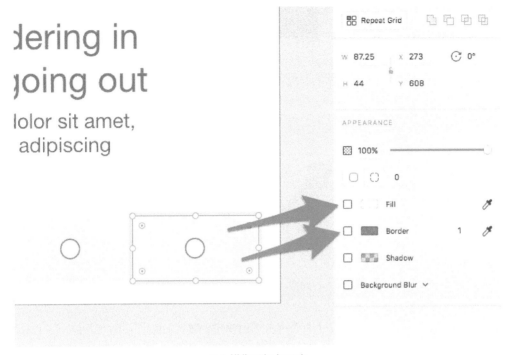

5-7. Hiding the bounds

Now you can see the navbar background clearly, but the bounds are still there, even if they are essentially hidden now.

Oh, and did you notice? All instances of the bottom nav component remain visually consistent with one another, even though you've only edited *one* of the instances. This is how symbols save us bundles of time, and offer us the peace of mind that we're maintaining consistency. It's a win-win situation.

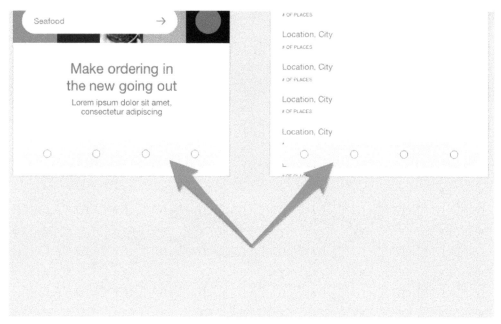

5-8. Visual consistency achieved

 We'll Leave the Icons for Now

Don't worry about the navbar icons — we'll tackle icon design in the next chapter as we learn about designing with vectors.

Unlinking An Instance From a Symbol

You can unlink an instance by **right-clicking** on it and selecting *Ungroup Symbol*. Note that this will not revert it back to any previous state — it will just not be linked to a symbol anymore, and you'll be able to edit it independently again.

Automating Content With Repeat Grids

We learned about repeat grids — and how we can use them to repeat design components horizontally and vertically — back in chapter two. Now let's discover how repeat grids can be useful in the high-fidelity prototyping stage as we add content to our design.

By dragging and dropping images and text files from our local computer, we can insert content into repeat grids with very little effort. If a component was tiled 20 times using a repeat grid, you would be able to drag 20 images into the grid at once, and Adobe XD would assign one of those images to each tile.

Let's take our list of search results for example — we could insert one background image into each result, all at once.

What Happens With Unused Images?

If the number of imported images outweighs the number of tiles, the extra images will remain unused. If the number of tiles outweighs the number of images being imported, Adobe XD will reuse already-imported images, resulting in duplicates.

Let's start by importing some images.

More Color Hints

Repeat grids are also outlined in green when selected, as editing one item in a repeat grid affects the other items.

Drag and Drop Image Import

Before we can mass-import images via drag and drop, we first need to ensure that all the images exist in the same location on our local computer. For the sake of this tutorial, you'll find example images you can use in the source files.

Locate the search result images within the source files, and use **Cmd + A (Ctrl + A** in Windows) to select all the images at once. Now drag them into the repeat grid in the *Search Results* artboard. When the background layer is highlighted, simply drop the images, and watch as Adobe XD automatically assigns one image for each instance of the background layer.

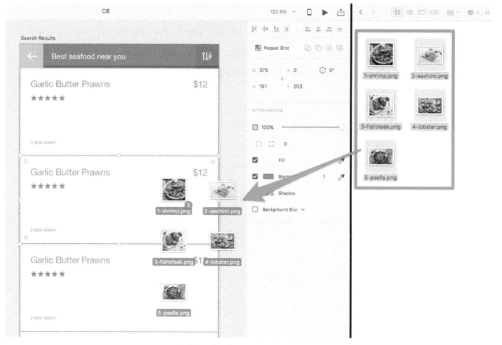

5-9. Dragging images onto the canvas

You should end up with something like this:

5-10. Mass-importing images

Drag and Drop Text Import

We can also import *written* content into the design using the same method. Ordinarily, we would insert written content by copying and pasting (usually delivered by the client or marketing team), but with Adobe XD we can drop text files containing the written content straight into the canvas.

It should be noted that each text layer requires its own text file. For instance, you would have one text file containing the written content for all item names, and another text file containing the written content for all item costs (I'm using the list of search results from our app as an example here).

Each value should appear on a new line. So a text file containing the item costs would look like this:

```
$19
$28
$17
$34
$48
```

Dragging and dropping text files is something that, at least to my knowledge, no other design app has done before. I was quite impressed when I discovered the ability to do this!

Before we begin importing some written content into our design, let's quickly style this search result component so our text layers are more visible when we drag the content in.

Styling the Search Result Grid

Begin by tweaking two styles on the rectangle shapes (which now use our imported images as backgrounds). Make the *Opacity* **60%** and remove the *Border* by unchecking it.

5-11. Styling the backgrounds

Now switch to the *Artboard* and use a *Fill* of **#000** to mimic the effect of having a black overlay on our background images. This will add more contrast to the text content when we add it.

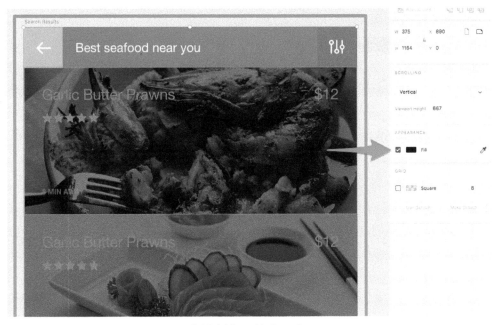

5-12. Adding a black overlay

Almost there — add two more styles:

 All text layers: *Fill* — **#FFFFFF**

All star shapes: *Fill* — **#E5B72B**

Maintaining Consistency

Just like with symbols, every instance in the repeat grid is visually consistent (apart from the content, of course).

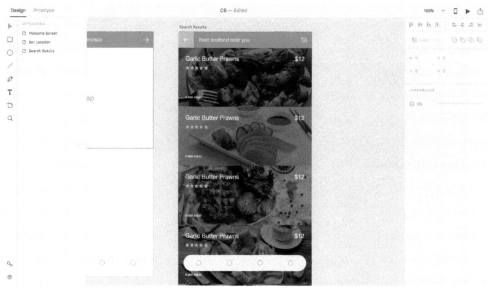

5-13. Grids are consistent

Importing the Text Content Into the Grid

As before, locate the text file in the source files. If you open the file, you'll notice it looks like this:

```
Garlic Butter Prawns
Salmon Sashimi
Flounder Amandine & Frites
Louisiana Seafood Boil
Seafood Paella
```

As you can see, each dish name should appear on a separate line, and the text file *must* be .txt format (not .rtf).

Drag the text file into the dish title text layer.

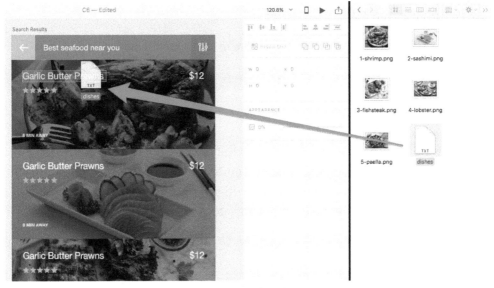

5-14. Dragging text into the canvas

You'll notice that Adobe XD has distributed one line from the text file to each instance of the dish title text layer.

5-15. Importing text content

Cycling Through Text

Should the text file not have enough lines of content to fill the repeat grid, it will cycle back to the first line.

Fast Forward

Fast forward two very short minutes — I've styled the repeat grid in the *Set Location* artboard, added some content, and imported a map image into the largest rectangle (drag-and-drop import works anywhere, not just repeat grids!). Apart from some icons, our mini-mockup is looking very much complete!

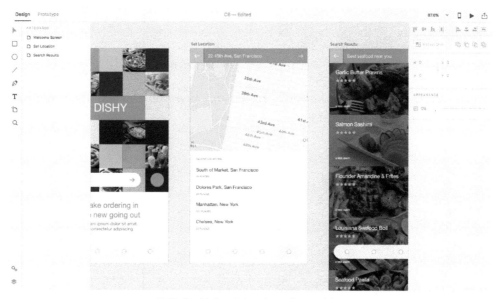

5-16. Our hi-fi prototype is nearly complete

Next: Designing Icons and Exporting

In the next chapter, we'll learn about the fine art of drawing vector shapes to create unique icons and illustrations. We'll finish off our high-fidelity screens by designing the icons, then we'll learn about exporting icons and other image assets.

Chapter

6

Designing Icons and Exporting

Back when we were low-fidelity prototyping, I (on the sly) inserted some icons into the design to add some clarity to our somewhat basic-looking wireframe. In this chapter, we'll learn how to design some of those icons from scratch. We'll explore the delicate art of icon design, as well as learn about the export feature, which allows us to ready our image assets for the developers, who will then implement them into the coded app.

Designing icons can be a difficult task, depending on what you're trying to accomplish. A slightly odd-looking shape might be easy enough to draw, but a complex icon would require much more care. Many designers use existing icon sets downloaded from the internet for this very reason — it's easier and quicker.

That being said, there's a *very* high chance your design will end up using the same icons as countless other designs. While this isn't really a big deal (it saves bundles of time and billable hours for the client!), some designs require a more unique visual aesthetic. There are also designs that need an icon for an app-specific feature or a branded version of a common icon. So we'll learn how to design an icon from scratch — one search icon and one location icon.

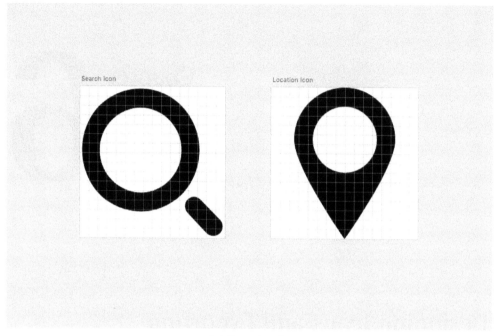

6-1. The end result

Let's start by designing a very simple search icon.

Designing a Search Icon

We'll begin by designing a search icon represented by a magnifying glass. This will consist of an ellipse shape (the circular glass itself) and a rectangle shape (the handle).

Creating an Artboard For The Search Icon

First we need a separate artboard for this icon, because we aren't going to create these icons directly in the design itself (that would make things a bit messy). When we're done, we'll have an icon that can be scaled to any size without losing quality (more on that later), then we'll copy a version of the icon into the design to see how it looks. Each icon will be approximately 16 x 16px, so create an artboard of that size.

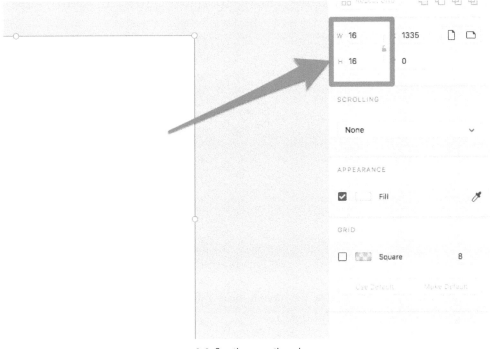

6-2. Creating an artboard

Activating Grids to Make Designing Easier

Grids can make the delicate art of designing icons *so* much easier, ensuring that our shapes and spacing are uniform. Grids are specifically offset from the top-left corner of the artboard, so by having each icon in its own artboard we can ensure our grids have a pre-determined amount of squares.

After making sure the artboard is selected, check the *Grid* checkbox in the inspector. You'll notice that, by default, lines are set to appear on the artboard every 8px. Since our artboard is only 16 x 16px, only two lines should be appearing right now.

6-3. Setting up grids

Change this setting to *1*. Now we have a more refined grid to work with, and can design our icons with careful detail.

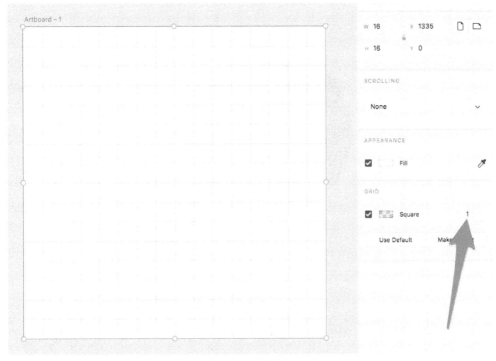

6-4. Changing the line settings

Designing the Search Icon

Let's create the two shapes that make up the search icon:

- Ellipse (**E**)
    - *Fill*: **#000**
    - *W* and *H*: **12**
    - *X* and *Y*: **0** (snapped to the top-left)
- Rectangle (**R**)
    - *Fill*: **#000**
    - *W*: **2**
    - *H*: **7**
    - *X* and *Y*: **10**
    - *Rotation*: **315°**
    - *Corner Radius*: **1**

You should have something like this:

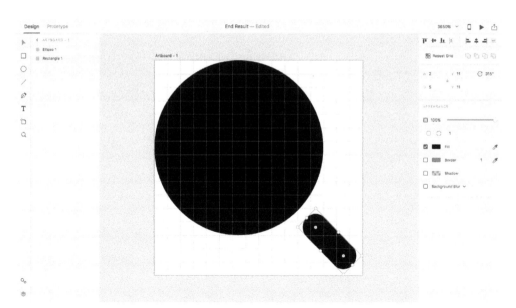

6-5. Building a rough base

I know what you're thinking — the circle shape is undesirably blocked out. We need to carve a smaller circle out of the larger circle, and that's where *boolean operations* can be useful.

A boolean operation combines two or more layers together to create a new shape. There are four types of boolean operations, and the one we need right now is called *Subtract*. We want to create a smaller ellipse shape and use it like a stencil to subtract from the larger ellipse. Let's do this now.

 ### This Is Similar To Pathfinder in Illustrator

If you're coming from an Adobe Illustrator background, you may be used to combining shapes using the Pathfinder features. Boolean operations are pretty much the same thing.

Start by creating a new ellipse shape:

- *W* and *H*: **9**
- *X* and *Y*: **2**
- *Fill*: **anything** (you'll see why shortly)

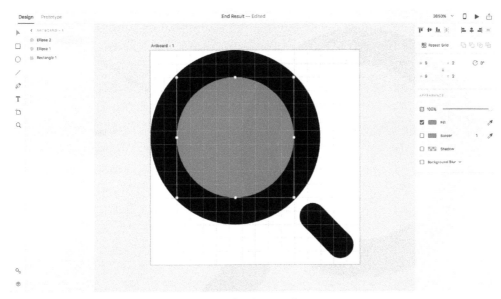

6-6. Creating a mask

We'll use this ellipse shape as a mask (or a stencil, if that term makes more sense to you). Now we'll complete a boolean operation (the Subtract operation, to be specific) to cut a hole out of the larger ellipse, using this mask/stencil.

Select both ellipse shapes, and select the Subtract boolean operation from the inspector. It won't actually say Subtract, but if you're at all unsure, the tooltip will help.

You can also use the very handy keyboard shortcut **Cmd + Option + S (Ctrl + Alt + S** in Windows).

You should notice that the mask ellipse has been used to cut a hole in the larger ellipse, and in the layer list, both layers have been combined into a single object called *Subtraction 1*.

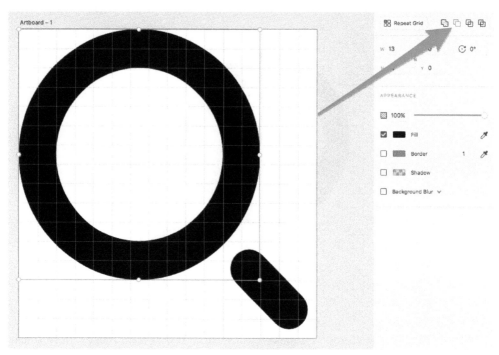

6-7. Our first icon is complete

You should also notice that the styles of the mask are irrelevant — when the layers are combined, the object inherits the styles from the layer lowest in the layer hierarchy.

 The Mask Layer Needs to be Above the Layer That's Being Operated On

Just like you were physically using a stencil in the real world, the mask layer should be *above* the layer that you want to subtract from. If it isn't *immediately* above, Adobe XD will automatically drag the layer further down the hierarchy.

You won't need to do anything in this case, but if for any reason you're not achieving the desired results, carefully rearrange the layers in the layer list before you select the boolean operation (a simple **Command/Ctrl + Z** will undo the operation if you make a mistake, don't worry).

Our first icon is complete!

Boolean Operations

We can create entirely unique shapes by using these boolean operations, as we did only moments ago when we carved a shape out of another shape. In the following examples, I'll use two ellipse shapes to re-demonstrate the Subtract operation, and also show you what the other operations can be accomplished.

All boolean operations are non-destructive. By non-destructive, I mean that we can **double-click** on the combined shape (in the layer list, or on the canvas directly) to resume editing the individual shapes even *after* the operation has completed.

Add and Subtract are the two boolean operations you'll use the most. But for the sake of clarity (since the inspector doesn't display any icon labels), the operations appear in this order, from left to right: Add, Subtract, Intersect, Exclude.

We'll start with Add.

Add Operation

Add combines two or more shapes into a single shape.

After selecting two or more shapes at once, use the keyboard shortcut **Cmd + Option + U (Ctrl + Alt + U** in Windows) to combine them using the Add boolean operation.

Before:

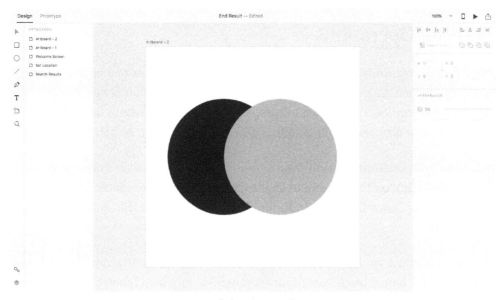

6-8. Before the operation

After:

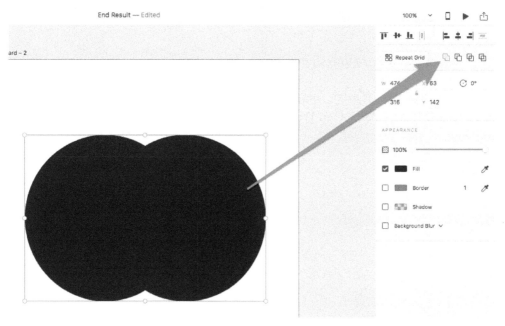

6-9. After the operation

"Wait, if various layers are combined, and they all have styles, which styles does the combined shape inherit?"

Well, as we saw when we used the Subtract operation on the search icon, the layer lowest in the layer hierarchy will be used as a base, and the combined shape will inherit the styles of this layer.

Before we move on, combine the layers that make up our search icon into a single object using the Add operation, then reposition the combined object into the center of the artboard.

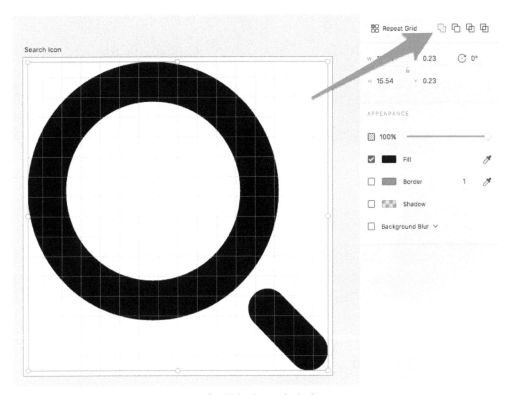

6-10. Combining into a single shape

Subtract Operation

We already explored the Subtract operation, but for completeness I'll explain it in more detail here.

Subtract does the complete opposite to Add. The layer that appears lowest in the layer hierarchy is used as the base, and any other shapes merged into it via a Subtract operation cut into this base like a stencil, "subtracting" from it. In the example below, I'm using an ellipse to subtract from another ellipse to create a crescent moon shape.

As you did with the Add operation, select the layers you want to merge, then click the subtract icon in the inspector, or use the keyboard shortcut **Cmd + Option + S (Ctrl + Alt + S** in Windows). You should have something like this:

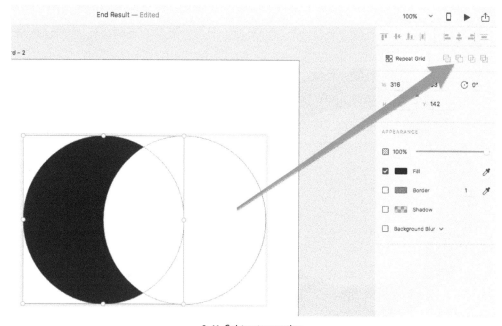

6-11. Subtract operation

Intersect Operation

Let's say you have two shapes that overlap each other. If you use the Intersect operation, only the area where the two shapes intersect/overlap will be visible. Keyboard shortcut: **Cmd + Option + I (Ctrl + Alt + I** in Windows).

In the case of these two overlapping ellipse shapes, you would end up with something like this:

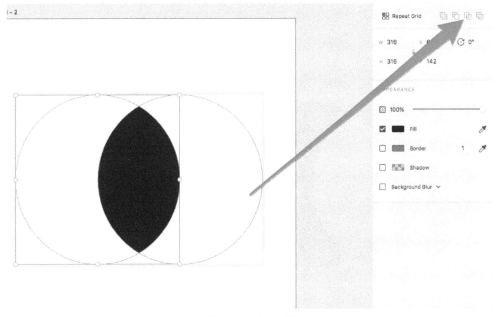

6-12. Intersect operation

Exclude Operation

This is the opposite of Intersect. After the selected layers are combined using the Exclude operation, you're left with the areas of the combined shape, where the individual shapes *aren't* overlapping. Keyboard shortcut: **Cmd + Option + X** (**Ctrl + Alt + X** in Windows).

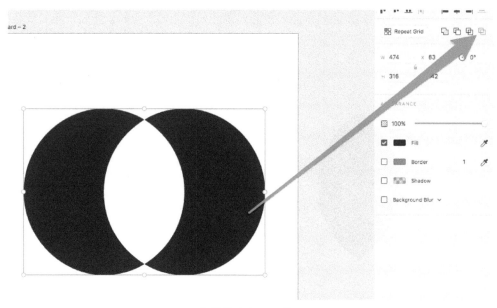

6-13. Exclude operation

Editing Vector Paths

Adobe XD is a vector app, so all text and shape layers are vectors. This means we can scale objects up and down without losing quality (a benefit that raster images do not have).

Vectors are comprised of *paths* that are connected via *points* at certain intervals. By adjusting these points, we can change the direction of each path, and ultimately, the overall outline of the shape. A *vector path* is a generated outline consisting of smooth, math-defined vector lines, rather than raster (bitmap) dots, making them fully resolution-independent.

In this next exercise we'll edit a simple ellipse into a location icon by manipulating its vector qualities.

Designing a Location Pin Icon

Create another 16 x 16px artboard and check the *Grid* checkbox once again. After switching the spacing to **1**, hit the adjacent *Make Default* button so we don't have to do this every time. Now create an ellipse shape and apply the follow styles:

- *Fill*: **#000**
- *W* and *H*: **11**
- *X*: **2.5**
- *Y*: **0**
- *Border*: uncheck this

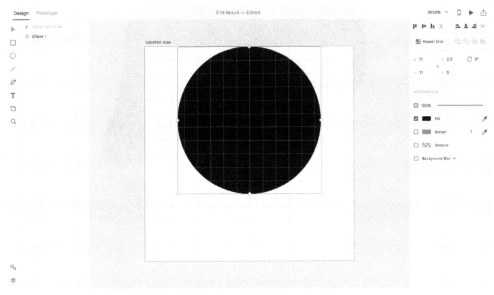

6-14. Halfway there already

Next, **double-click** on the ellipse to enter *vector mode*, where you'll notice that this shape has four points (one each at the north, east, south and west edges). These are more specifically known as *anchor points* or *anchors*, and you can drag them to manipulate the core structure of the shape.

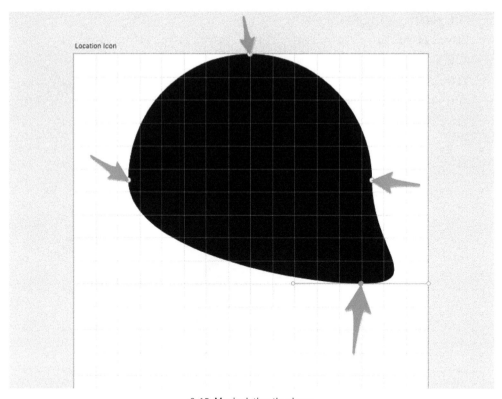

6-15. Manipulating the shape

Anchor and Control Points

When you select an anchor, you'll see two other handles appear on either side, connected to it via a line. These two handles are called *control points*, and they can be used to adjust the curvature of the path between a) the currently selected anchor, and b) its neighboring anchors.

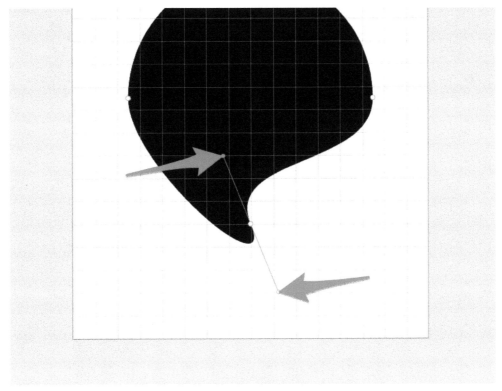

6-16. Moving the control handles

In short:

- *Anchor point*: moving this changes the mould of the shape
- *Control point*: moving this changes the curvature of the *paths* that make up the shape

By default, anchors are mirrored. When you move one control handle, the other handle moves in the opposite direction symmetrically (resulting in a smooth curve effect).

In order to move a control handle *asymmetrically* (meaning, without the opposite handle automatically mimicking its behaviour), hold **Option/Alt** while you move it. When you hold **Option/Alt**, the control handle can be moved independently, allowing for the possibility to create asymmetric shapes.

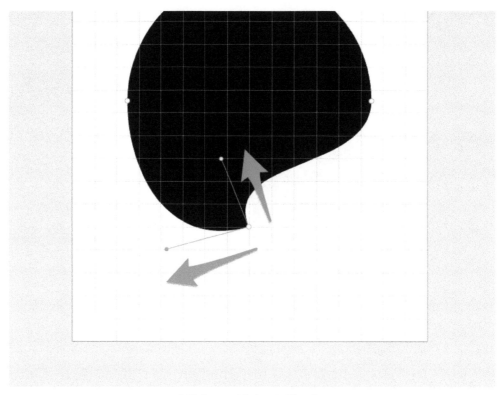

6-17. Asymmetrical control handles

 Play Around!

With the knowledge of anchors and controls fresh in your mind, I'd advise you to play around with some shapes, as this is the best way of learning how to draw vectors quickly.

Converting Mirrored Points to Straight Points

Paths are curved by default, as we've learned, and the control handles allow us to adjust those curves. By **double-clicking** on the anchor, we can convert this mirrored anchor to a straight anchor. Straight anchors *do not* have control handles because there's no curvature to control. **Double-click** on the bottom-most anchor to convert it, then drag it to the bottom-center of the artboard, using the *Grid* to achieve the accuracy required. Grids are handy for more complex icons.

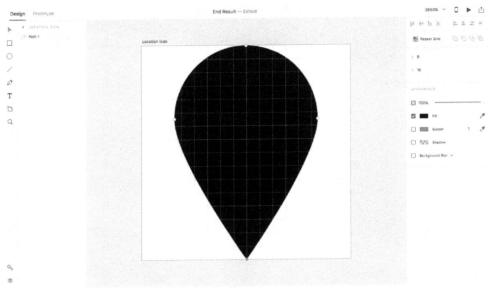

6-18. Converting anchors

Completing the Icon with a Boolean Operation

As we did with the search icon, we can use a Subtract operation to cut a hole in the middle of the location icon. Create an ellipse shape with the following styles:

- *W* and *H*: **7**
- *X*: **4.5**
- *Y*: **2**

Remember, the *Fill* and *Border* styles have zero relevance, as the eventual combined shape will inherit the styles from the base layer (icon), not the mask layer (the ellipse).

6-19. Creating an ellipse mask

Select both layers then hit the keyboard shortcut for Subtract, which is **Cmd + Option + S** (**Ctrl + Alt + S** in Windows).

6-20. Performing the operation

Our second icon is now complete.

Drawing Vectors with Keyboard Shortcuts

As usual, there are a few keyboard shortcuts that can help us design faster, and with more accuracy. Let's take a look!

- **Shift (hold)**: Snap handles at 15° increments
- **Alt/Option (hold)**: Move control handle asymmetrically
- **Shift + Alt/Option (hold)**: Both of the above at once
- **Backspace/Delete**: Delete anchor

Pen Tool

Sometimes, shape manipulations and boolean operations alone won't help you achieve the level of detail you desire. Occasionally, you might need to illustrate a vector from scratch. This is a whole other skill in itself, and why many designers find it easier (and far less time-consuming) to download and implement a ready-made icon set (which is perfectly acceptable!).

 Finding Icons

Creative Market[1], Icons8[2], Iconfinder[3], UI8[4], The Noun Project[5] and Dribbble[6] are brilliant resources for finding complete (and attractive) icon sets.

Designing a vector from scratch really isn't that different from what we've been doing in this chapter. The only difference is you'll need to use the *Pen* tool to draw shapes. However, if you know how to work the anchor and control handles (which you do, now!), then you know how to use the pen tool.

Press **P** and click anywhere on the artboard to create an anchor, then click somewhere on the artboard to create another anchor, establishing a *Path* between the two.

[1.] https://creativemarket.com/graphics/icons
[2.] https://icons8.com/
[3.] https://www.iconfinder.com
[4.] https://ui8.net/categories/icons
[5.] https://thenounproject.com/
[6.] https://dribbble.com/search?q=download+icons

Keep clicking until you come full circle to the original anchor, then *close the path* by clicking on the first anchor created. Paths can be split by clicking on them, resulting in a new anchor being created underneath the mouse cursor. Press **Delete** (**Backspace** in Windows) to delete anchors. It's simple in theory, but it requires a lot of practice in reality.

Using Other Apps to Create Your Vectors

Compared with a tool like Illustrator, Adobe XD is pretty basic when it comes to drawing vectors. Many designers would agree that using Illustrator for complex illustrations is much better. Luckily, copying and pasting vectors from Adobe Illustrator to Adobe XD works flawlessly. You can also copy or drag SVG files from your computer into Adobe XD — even those exported from Sketch.

Copying Icons into the Design Itself

Next, copy and paste the icons into the design itself to make sure they look right (sometimes, you may need to tweak the icon a little more, utilising symbols to maintain consistency).

Here's what the final design should look like, complete with all icons and screens (and, as usual, you can find the full design file in the support files, so you can take a closer look):

6-21. Final result

Exporting Image Assets

Let's begin exporting these icons, so the developers (let's assume we have developers!) can begin implementing them into the coded application. The file format, and the size we need to export these icons, depends on whether we're designing a website, an iOS app, or an Android app. We're designing an iOS app, but we'll cover web and Android, too.

Start by selecting one or more icons, then hit **Cmd + E** (**Ctrl + E** in Windows) to begin the export workflow. Let's run through the settings available, and learn which ones are required for the different operating systems available today.

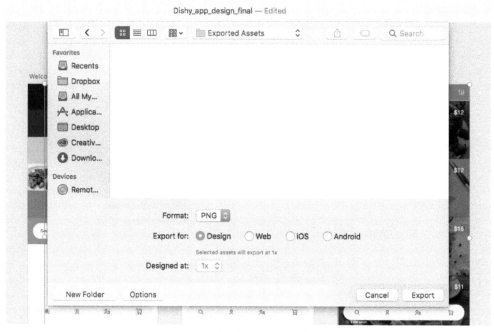

6-22. Starting the export workflow

Image Formats

Format specifies which file format the selected objects will be exported as — this depends on whether you're designing for the web, or for an iOS/Android app. We have three options:

- *PNG*: A bitmap format that cannot be scaled without losing quality; for websites and iOS/Android operating systems

- *SVG*: A vector format that *can* be scaled without losing quality; for the web only (we'll discuss why shortly)

- *PDF*: An uncommon vector format for iOS/Android

Even though device resolution (ie, display size/quality) varies from device to device, PNG formats are the norm for mobile devices, **not** vector formats such as SVG. I'll explain why.

Resolution and Platform

Device resolution is a very difficult concept to understand at first — PaintCode's[7] visual explanation of iPhone resolutions is the easiest to understand (and the best to refer back to later)[8]. For now, let me explain the basic concept so you know which settings to choose when exporting your designs. Since we're designing an iOS app, I'll use iOS as an example to start with.

When the iPhone was first released, it didn't include any *Retina* technology, so we exported our designs **@1x**. The iPhone 4 included the Retina technology, which doubled the amount of *pixels* on the screen, even though the screen didn't physically increase in size. This meant we needed to export our assets at double the size (**@2x**), resulting in better display quality.

Later, the resolution increased even further with the release of the iPhone 6 Plus, so we needed to export images **@3x** (ie, the display had three times as many pixels).

"But what if I'm designing for various iPhone devices? PNG is not a vector format, so the images would be blurry when scaling up and down for the different device resolutions!"

Well, this brings me back to image formats. Because vectors have to be mathematically rendered (this is what makes them scalable), this is very resource-intensive on the mobile device.

Since PNG files do not have this issue, and iOS *preloads* PNG files before launching the app, this isn't resource-intensive at all. If we export the PNG files at **@1x, @2x** *and* **@3x**, iOS will then serve whichever version is relevant to the device, resulting in high-quality, device-specific images that don't have be mathematically rendered each time they appear. This is the most-common and most-recommended method of exporting assets.

"What about JPG files?"

[7.] https://www.paintcodeapp.com/news/ultimate-guide-to-iphone-resolutions
[8.] https://developer.android.com/guide/practices/screens_support.html is similar resource for Android devices

Since JPG formats don't support alpha-transparency (whereas PNG does), and file size isn't a concern for native apps, we don't typically export image assets in JPG format for native apps — Adobe XD doesn't support it. We do, however, still use JPG on the web because of its ability to be compressed into a smaller file size, so we can expect Adobe XD to introduce JPG exports soon.

"Why are PDFs uncommon?"

Mobile apps (both iOS and Android) will convert PDFs to PNG at runtime — the benefit is that you'll have fewer assets to export (because PDFs are scalable), but in exchange for a slow, more resource-intensive app. I would avoid this method in all cases.

Now let's explore the two remaining settings:

- *Export for*:

  - *Design*: PNGs **@1x**
  - *Web*: PNGs **@1x and @2x**
  - *iOS*: PNGs **@1x, @2x and @3x**
  - *Android*: PNGs at **ldpi, mdpi, hdpi, xhdpi, xxhdpi and xxxhdpi** (Android has a wider variety of device resolutions and uses different terms to differentiate between them)

- *Designed at*: This is the resolution at which the assets were designed. We designed our assets **@1x** — this is the default option, the resolution at which the artboards are created.

I would highly advise that you design **@1x**, as this makes it super-easy to scale up image assets to **@2x and @3x**. Similarly, you should choose **100% - mdpi** for Android designs, as this is the default resolution for Android artboards.

For our design, choose the **iOS** and **1x** options, then hit the *Export* button to export the assets to the chosen location.

And we're done!

It's a Wrap

You did it! You learned how to design user interfaces in Adobe XD! You visualised your idea in a low-fidelity mockup, learned how to ask for feedback, then designed the screens to completion – and topped it off with some icons. And hopefully it didn't even take you that long! Don't forget to check out the appendix at the end of this book, where we'll recap all the macOS and Windows keyboard shortcuts (there's a handy PDF cheatsheet for you to download as well, in case you forget them later).

We'll also revisit some of those repetitive tasks that can be time-consuming if you're not using the keyboard shortcuts.

I'll see you there!

Appendix A: Accelerating Workflows with Keyboard Shortcuts

In this final chapter we'll explore how keyboard shortcuts can accelerate our prototyping workflow. We learned several of these shortcuts throughout the book, but we'll recap all of them here, as well as learn about any that we missed along the way. On top of that, we'll explore certain repetitive tasks and see how we can speed them up using shortcuts.

Keyboard Shortcut Workflows

We'll start with those repetitive (or easy-to-forget) tasks.

Quickly Reorganise Your Workspace

Switching up your workspace is super-easy. Here are the three keyboard shortcuts that will speed up your workflow.

- Switch Workspace: **Ctrl + Tab** (**Ctrl + Tab** in Windows)
- Switch to Layers Panel: **Cmd + Y** (macOS only)
- Switch to Symbol Library: **Cmd + Shift + Y** (macOS only)

Masking Layers

Mask objects by selecting any number of objects on the canvas and using the keyboard shortcut **Cmd + Shift + M** (**Ctrl + Shift + M** in Windows). The object highest in the object hierarchy (the object that appears on top of the others) will be the mask, and any other layers will be masked underneath.

After this, the mask can be moved around independently as a single object, although you can **double-click** the mask in the layer list to open it and make changes to the masked objects.

Any styles associated with the mask will be voided.

Option/Alt

In Adobe XD, **Option-Hold** (**Alt-Hold** in Windows) has multiple uses depending on the context in which it is used.

Hold **Option** or **Alt**...

- After selecting an object to activate *Smart Guides*
- After selecting a *Control Point* to move it asymmetrically
- While drawing or resizing an object to draw/resize from the center of the object, instead of from the mouse cursor
- While dragging to *copy and paste* an object

Shift

Shift has even more uses than **Option**!

Hold **Shift**...

- While moving a *Control Point* to allow only angle values that are 15°, or a multiple of 15° (15°, 30°, 45°, 90°, 180°, etc)
- While moving an *Anchor Point* to allow only angle values that are 15°, or a multiple of 15° (15°, 30°, 45°, 90°, 180°, etc)
- While drawing or resizing an object to draw/resize with the aspect ratio maintained (also known as "constrain") — add **Shift** to the mix to constrain from the center of the object
- While rotating objects to rotate angles by multiples of 15° only
- While rotating lines to rotate angles by multiples of 45° only

Keyboard Shortcuts for macOS

General Shortcuts

Note: These shortcuts are standard with most macOS apps.

- Quit App: **Cmd + Q**
- Hide App Window: **Cmd + H**

- Hide Other App Windows: **Cmd + Option + H**
- Minimise App Window: **Cmd + M**

Basic Commands

- Undo: **Cmd + Z**
- Redo: **Cmd + Shift + Z**
- Cut: **Cmd + X**
- Copy: **Cmd + C**
- Paste: **Cmd + V**
- Duplicate: **Cmd + D**
- Delete: **Delete**
- Select All: **Cmd + A**
- Deselect All: **Cmd + Shift + A**

Workspace and Canvas Commands

- Zoom In: **Cmd and +** (or **Option + two-finger swipe up**)
- Zoom Out: **Cmd and -** (or **Option + two-finger swipe down**)
- Zoom to Fit: **Cmd + 0**
- Zoom 100%: **Cmd + 1**
- Zoom 200%: **Cmd + 2**
- Zoom to Selection: **Cmd + 3**
- Show Artboard Grid: **Cmd + '**
- Enter Full Screen: **Cmd + Ctrl + F**
- Switch Workspace: **Ctrl + Tab**
- Switch to Layers Panel: **Cmd + Y**
- Switch to Symbol Library: **Cmd + Shift + Y**

Switch Between Tools

- Select: **V**
- Rectangle: **R**
- Ellipse: **E**
- Line: **L**
- Pen: **P**

- Text: **T**
- Artboard: **A**

Export, Share and Preview Commands

- Export Asset: **Cmd + E**
- Import Asset: **Cmd + Shift + I**
- Share Prototype: **Cmd + Shift + E**
- Preview Prototype: **Cmd + Return**

Object Commands

- Group: **Cmd + G**
- Ungroup: **Cmd + Shift + G**
- Make Symbol: **Cmd + K**
- Make Repeat Grid: **Cmd + R**
- Mask with Shape: **Cmd + Shift + M**
- Lock Object (object cannot be moved/styled): **Cmd + L**
- Hide Object (object will not be visible): **Cmd + ;**

Rearrange Layer Hierarchy

- Bring Forward: **Cmd +]**
- Send Backward: **Cmd + [**
- Bring to Front: **Cmd + Shift +]**
- Send to Back: **Cmd + Shift + [**

Align Layers

- Left: **Cmd + Ctrl + ←**
- Right: **Cmd + Ctrl + →**
- Top: **Cmd + Ctrl + ↑**
- Bottom: **Cmd + Ctrl + ↓**
- Center (horizontally): **Cmd + Ctrl + C**
- Middle (vertically): **Cmd + Ctrl + M**

Distribute Layers

- Horizontal: **Cmd + Ctrl + H**
- Vertical: **Cmd + Ctrl + V**

Change Font Styles

- Bold: **Cmd + B**
- Italic: **Cmd + I**

Boolean Operation Commands

- Add: **Cmd + Option + U**
- Subtract: **Cmd + Option + S**
- Intersect: **Cmd + Option + I**
- Exclude Overlap: **Cmd + Option + X**
- Convert to Path: **Cmd + 8**

Drawing Commands

- Pen Tool: **P**
- Convert Straight to Mirrored Point: **Double-Click**
- Asymmetric Point: **Option-Hold**
- Snap Control Point Angle: **Shift-Hold**
- Snap Anchor Point Angle: **Shift-Hold**

Miscellaneous Operations

- Draw/Resize From Center: **Option-Hold**
- Constrain (Maintain Aspect Ratio): **Shift-Hold**
- Constrain From Center: **Option + Shift**
- Constrain Rotate (15°): **Shift-Hold**
- Line Constrain Rotate (45°): **Shift-Hold**
- Smart Guides: **Option-Hold**
- Edit Text: **Return**
- Copy-Paste Object: **Option + Drag**

Direct Select (Click-Through Group): **Cmd + Left-Click**

Keyboard Shortcuts for Windows

General Shortcuts

- Quit App: **Alt + F4**
- Minimise App Window : **WIN ↓**

Basic Commands

- Undo: **Ctrl + Z**
- Redo: **Ctrl + Shift + Z**
- Cut: **Ctrl + X**
- Copy: **Ctrl + C**
- Paste: **Ctrl + V**
- Duplicate: **Ctrl + D**
- Delete: **Delete**
- Select All: **Ctrl + A**
- Deselect All: **Ctrl + Shift + A**

Workspace and Canvas Commands

- Zoom In: **Ctrl and +**
- Zoom Out: **Ctrl and -**
- Zoom to Fit: **Ctrl + 0**
- Zoom 100%: **Ctrl + 1**
- Zoom 200%: **Ctrl + 2**
- Zoom to Selection: **Ctrl + 3**
- Pan: **Spacebar**
- Show Artboard Grid: **Ctrl + '**
- Switch Workspace: **Ctrl + Tab**

Switch Between Tools

- Select: **V**

- Rectangle: **R**
- Ellipse: **E**
- Line: **L**
- Pen: **P**
- Text: **T**
- Artboard: **A**

Export, Share and Preview Commands

- Export Asset: **Ctrl + E**
- Import Asset: **Ctrl + Shift + I**
- Share Prototype: **Ctrl + Shift + E**
- Preview Prototype: **Ctrl + Enter**

Object Commands

- Group: **Ctrl + G**
- Ungroup: **Ctrl + Shift + G**
- Make Repeat Grid: **Ctrl + R**

- Mask with Shape: **Ctrl + Shift + M**
- Lock Object (object cannot be moved/styled): **Ctrl + L**

Rearrange Layer Hierarchy

- Bring Forward: **Ctrl +]**
- Send Backward: **Ctrl + [**
- Bring to Front: **Ctrl + Shift +]**
- Send to Back: **Ctrl + Shift + [**

Align Layers

- Left: **Ctrl + Shift + ←**
- Right: **Ctrl + Shift + →**
- Top: **Ctrl + Shift + ↑**
- Bottom: **Ctrl + Shift + ↓**

- Center (Horizontally): **Shift + C**
- Middle (Vertically): **Shift + M**

Distribute Layers

- Horizontal: **Ctrl + Shift + H**
- Vertical: **Ctrl + Shift + V**

Change Font Styles

- Bold: **Ctrl + B**
- Italic: **Ctrl + I**

Boolean Operation Commands

- Add: **Ctrl + Alt + U**
- Subtract: **Ctrl + Alt + S**
- Intersect: **Ctrl + Alt + I**
- Exclude Overlap: **Ctrl + Alt + X**
- Convert to Path: **Ctrl + 8**

Drawing Commands

- Pen Tool: **P**
- Convert Straight →← Mirrored Point: **Double-Click**
- Asymmetric Point: **Option-Hold**
- Snap Control Point Angle: **Shift-Hold**
- Snap Anchor Point Angle: **Shift-Hold**

Miscellaneous Operations

- Draw/Resize From Center: **Alt-Hold**
- Constrain (Maintain Aspect Ratio): **Shift-Hold**
- Constrain From Center: **Shift + Alt**
- Constrain Rotate (15°): **Shift-Hold**
- Line Constrain Rotate (45°): **Shift-Hold**

- Smart Guides: **Alt-Hold**
- Edit Text: **Enter**
- Copy and Paste Object: **Alt + Drag**
- Direct Select (Click-Through Group): **Ctrl + Left-Click**